How To Lose Your Shirt In Real Estate

Twenty-Six Common Mistakes To Avoid

TRACY A. SANDBERG

ITP Inc.
Distributed by Kampmann & Co.

Published by

Investment and Tax Publications, Inc.

P.O. Box 1201

Orem, Utah 84057

Distributed by Kampmann & Co.
New York (212-685-2928)

"This publication is designed to provide accurate and authoritative information in regard to the subject matter covered. It is sold with the understanding that the publisher is not engaged in rendering legal, accounting, or other professional service. If legal advice or other expert assistance is required, the services of a competent professional person should be sought."

From a declaration or principles jointly adopted by a committee of the American Bar Association and committee of the Publishers' Association.

ISBN   0910019-16-9

ABOUT THE AUTHOR

Through years of experience as an investor, realtor, trainer, lecturer and author, Mr. Sandberg has developed a unique ability to grasp confusing, technical real estate concepts and present them in a simplified form for use by the investor—whether experienced or novice.

His practical knowledge comes from his own experience. He acquired, managed and sold properties of several different types, using several different investment strategies, and experiencing varying degrees of success. Some projects were absolute disasters, but Mr. Sandberg was able to analyze each success and failure to discover why they happened. The result is this practical guidebook, **How to Lose Your Shirt in Real Estate** — *26 Common Mistakes to Avoid.*

A great believer in real estate, he became a realtor and despite the dreary real estate atmosphere of 1979-1981, he closed 1.2 million dollars in ratified transactions in his first six months as an agent.

He now shares with you his insights and recommendations through his many seminars and works now in print.

To my wife, Lynn who patiently shares my triumphs and failures, my prudent acts and my mistakes.

CONTENTS

FOREWORD

With this volume I am pleased to welcome Tracy Sandberg to Investment and Tax Publications' family of distinguished authors. As presented in this volume, his insight into the more devastating problems that investors periodically encounter will save much aggravation and loss for many investors nationwide. This book is an important addition to the library of any investor—advanced or novice. You will find this work to be ideal as a companion volume to Mr. Sandberg's other more technical books and to the technical books of other authors.

His seminars on several different real estate investment topics have been well received and he is becoming well known as an educator. Some reasons for his growing popularity will become apparent as you read **How to Lose Your Shirt in Real Estate — Twenty-six Common Mistakes to Avoid.**

I have a saying framed and hanging on my office wall, *"Anyone can learn from experience, the wise man learns from someone else's experience."* Indeed, the goal of ITP is to spread experience around and invite all investors to be wise by learning from someone else's experience. This book is such an opportunity. I invite you to read it and learn.

Sincerely,

Wade B. Cook

Chairman

Investment and Tax Publications, Inc.

PREFACE

One of the main concerns of the founding fathers of our nation was to preserve and protect the right of the individual to own property. Written into the Constitution were specific restrictions placed on the government against interfering with the rights of private ownership of land. This right to own real estate has been further protected and encouraged in later years by the structure of the tax system. More specifically, the government has actually encouraged people to own real estate for purposes of providing rental housing for others, and they've done this by offering tax benefits to those who are willing to buy and manage rental housing. Every person has the opportunity to profit by taking advantage of this system which is established for that purpose. The probability of success, then, in real estate investment has been heavily weighted by the government in favor of the investor. For this reason, I believe that success in an investment program in real estate will come by simply avoiding the big mistakes so commonly made. For the purpose of avoiding these mistakes, this book was written.

Many of you, who will be using the suggestions in this

book, will already have had some experience in purchasing or selling a home. It is crucial to your success as an investor to make clear the distinction between buying, holding, and selling investment property, and buying and selling the property in which you live. Simply stated, if you approach buying your first investment in the same manner in which you approached buying your own residence, the seeds are planted for failure.

The moment you have purchased your first investment property, you are in the real estate investment business. You, then are a **bus**iness person, and must conduct yourself as such. Your decisions will be business decisions; no longer dictated by personal likes and dislikes and no longer dictated by emotion, or urgency, or any other personal need. It will be required of you to become familiar with the instruments and the methods of conducting business, the reasonable expectations and the possible negative results of business ventures and how they impact on you personally. My lack of understanding of this very point contributed heavily to my early investment failures. And from those early experiences, I've designed this book to be a tool for avoiding mistakes which will cause failure in a governmental tax system that is favorably structured for your success.

I picture this work as a companion volume to other real estate investment books presently available. I owe much to those other authors whose writings encouraged me toward my first investment experience. I feel, however, that their books were significantly lacking in warnings of the dangers involved in this type of venture. They were insufficient in preparing me adequately for the realities of being an investor. They did not indicate what could go wrong or how to see problems coming. Perhaps this volume may fill that gap and further serve you by toning down your ardor, allowing you to approach investing in real estate more rationally and safely.

I am convinced your early investing experiences will be all the more rewarding for having read this book.

HOW TO LOSE
YOUR SHIRT
IN REAL ESTATE

Chapter 1

IF HE CAN DO IT, I CAN DO IT

I remember picking up my first book on real estate investing, reading how the author, in a penniless condition had borrowed $500, purchased real estate, managed it, and sold it at a profit; and by repeating that process, in a miraculously short period of time, launched himself into tremendous wealth. The basic plan was to buy a property, make some cosmetic improvements, raise the rents to the break-even point (or to a positive cash flow), hold the property for twelve months or so, and then sell it, taking a profit as a long term capital gain. The profits would be reinvested and the process repeated.

I was so excited! I firmly believed that if this person could do it, I could do it. I reasoned in my mind that I was in all probability, brighter than the person who wrote the book to begin with. I had money in my pocket to work with, and I had the advantage of his experience to guide me. I couldn't lose. So I determined to begin my brilliant investment career and launch myself into wealth.

NEGOTIATING

I immediately went out and negotiated with an owner who wanted to sell his rental property. We were living at this time in a $40,000 house—happy just to be able to make the payments. The property I was trying to buy was actually two buildings and the sale price was $125,000. The seller and I dickered back and forth for two full weeks on the exact terms of the sale, and I was shaking in my boots the entire time. Each time $125,000 began to sound like a lot of money to me, I'd excuse myself from talking with the gentleman and run home to read parts of that real estate book again. Re-enthused by the inevitability of success, and bolstered by the thought that if the author could do it, I could, I went back and continued negotiating.

I remember coming home the day we concluded the agreement. I was exhausted, but triumphant. I had actually succeeded in buying a sizeable chunk of rental property at a time when we could hardly afford the property we were living in. I actually bought it with no cash down and no income with which to qualify for such a purchase. I actually did what the author said could be done. The agreement was a triumph to me, but when I explained it to my wife she hit the ceiling. "One hundred twenty-five thousand dollars in debt?" I hadn't really thought of it that way.

Although she had read parts of the investment book that

had excited me and kept me motivated all this time, she hadn't gotten to the part that explained what a tremendous profit I was going to make in the future.

None-the-less, I proceeded, as prescribed, to make some minor cosmetic changes on the property and raise the rents. I soon discovered that the rents I could get for the apartments were not quite high enough to cover the payments I had to make. On top of that, there was no money at all available from other income for repairs and replacements. We succeeded, however, in holding the property for 12 months, but it nearly killed us in the process.

During that year I discovered that there were things the author of my real estate book forgot to tell me, like the fact that you can really hurt yourself by getting into a real estate investment without knowing what you are doing. You can lose your shirt!

OMISSION

He forgot to tell me that there were unplanned vacancies to plan on. He forgot to tell me that tenants would pay late with checks that bounce. He forgot to tell me about the extremely high utility bills, and numerous unexpected expenses and repairs. He forgot to tell me that on Christmas Eve at 11:00 p.m., I'd be called to come and fix someone's plumbing because they had neglected to tell me that the sinks and toilets had been overflowing for three days. He forgot to tell me that I'd have to evict tenants at great cost and hassle to me, and that once they moved, they'd take all my furniture with them.

I should have realized from the beginning that though the circumstances may be similar, *no two investors will have the same results.* Although I had learned a lot from another person's experiences, I learned from my own experiences that it is folly to expect to always have the same successes as others. The author plainly forgot to tell me of the various things that can go **wrong**, so I was unprepared to deal with them when they did.

My first mistake was the assumption that if he can do it, I can do it exactly the same way. "It ain't necessarily so."

Chapter 2

A PARTNER
CHOOSES YOU

Many first experiences in investment real estate involve a partner of one sort or another; someone who can share the initial expense, the liability, and eventually, the profits. This is a legitimate need, especially when limited experience and capital dictate that you find someone else to help out. You choose a partner to fill those needs. It may prove very helpful, however, to point out that your prospective partner also chooses a partner to fill *his* needs. You may be tempted to allow the promise of tremendous profit from the transaction to overshadow the inconveniences and possible hazards of having to work with a partner. But look closely at the needs of the person with whom you propose to do business.

The value of this counsel was dramatically pointed out to me one time prior to my real estate experience. My brother and I had been in another business for a relatively short period of time when we met a person who had been in the same business for years and years, and had just dissolved a relationship with his former partner. We proposed taking him on as a third partner in our business.

TRUST

He told us he had broken up with his last partner on less than favorable terms, due to the failings of that other partner. We, of course, believed him. We wanted to start this partnership on the right foot, and wanted trust to be the basis of the relationship.

After a short time of being in business together, he left the state unexpectedly with no forwarding address. My brother and I then started getting phone calls from suppliers who said we owed them money. It turned out that our partner had been running up debts all over town in the name of the partnership, and left us holding the bag. It took us several years to pay off all the debts he had charged to our account.

In the process of cleaning up the whole mess, we checked with his former partner who was a local resident. He revealed to us that their partnership had dissolved because this same person had done something similarly dishonest at that time. If we had just asked the right questions of the right people eight months earlier, it might have saved us a great deal of money and a lot of hassle.

My approach now to a partnership is suspicious by nature. In fact, I believe that anyone who would want me as a partner is exercising very poor judgment to begin with. I wouldn't join any club that would have me as a member, either. I say that facetiously, but I think the idea is worthy of consideration.

Look at it this way—if he is responding favorably to your proposal of partnership, he wants you to be his partner for one of four reasons: 1) Your experience, judgment and wisdom in the business would be an asset to him, 2) You're just a wonderful person and he would just love being affiliated with you, 3) You have money, assets, or property that he needs at this time, or 4) He has a tremendous amount of liability that he needs to spread around and you are available to take on some of it.

CLOSER LOOK AT POSSIBILITIES

Let's take a closer look at these possibilities. First of all, if a person is in business for himself, he's there because he wants to make his own decisions. He may not really want someone else's experience, judgment or wisdom to dictate what he does. Making decisions by committee is a very cumbersome way to do business, so it's unlikely that he wants your input. Certain occupations seem to breed this independence, or maybe independent people choose certain occupations that allow this freedom. At any rate, doctors, dentists, lawyers, and airline pilots (among others) are very difficult people to have as partners because they like to be in total control, whether they know anything about real estate, or not.

Don't count yourself out yet, however. He still might

want you for a partner because you are a great guy. If this is the case, you might like to skip ahead to chapter four.

All right, so he may really want you for your money and assets or he may want to dump liabilities on you. If he wants your money, he may be taking you along only because you come with the package. If there were any other way to get your money or assets he wouldn't trouble himself with the entanglements of a partnership. He may discover later on that there is some other way to get your money away from you, and attempt to do it.

What about his need to dump liabilities? I have run into people who are carrying around a tremendous load of liabilities that they need to spread around. If a partner wants you for this reason, he is trying to put his monkey on your back.

I don't mean to be unduly suspicious of people, but occasionally, some people find themselves, at least temporarily, in a position of extreme necessity. These same people are otherwise governed by the highest motives, but in the case of extreme desperation, they may find no other answer to their troubles than to take your money, put you into debt, and skip out of town. Before you go into any kind of a partnership agreement, check out the person, not just the transaction. Check into his past record, his past and present partners, and his present circumstances and needs. Then put your entire partnership agreement **in writing**; what duties each person will have, what responsibilities they will answer to, how the liabilities and profits will be divided and what will happen if one of the parties defaults in his or her responsibilities.

BUSINESS WITH ACQUAINTANCES

One time my wife and I were approached by an acquaintance, whom we had known through our church affiliation. He came to us saying that he needed a couple thousand dollars, and would cut us into an extremely profitable business opportunity dealing with real estate. Of course, we were acquaintances of his and he felt that we had a lot on the ball, and were bright enough to take advantage of this wonderful opportunity. We took a look at the transaction. It had a lot of promise, so we entered into a partnership. We provided ourselves, however, in this written partnership agreement, the option to back out under certain conditions, in which case our money would be returned. We carefully spelled out how the money would be used and how the property would be managed and eventually disposed of.

It didn't take long before we realized he wasn't doing what he said he would do. It turned out that he needed the money to pay off certain personal liabilities. He was in trouble. The end result was that he was getting us into trouble too. If we had been wise enough to discover this need before we entered into the partnership, we could have saved ourselves much personal, financial, and emotional trauma.

Look for signs of desperation. Any indication of extreme urgency in a prospective partner's request is a tip-off that there's trouble brewing. An investor who is going under financially can take a lot of other people with him. There is a certain "point of no return" in a person's financial career, and once that point is reached, other people's money may not be able to save him. So getting involved at that point would only serve to spread the tragedy around.

No matter how good the transaction looks, if there's desperation or urgency involved, stay clear. I've seen investors who only deal in buying and selling deeds of trust turn down a one year, heavily discounted note netting almost a 100% return, because the deal was too good—the seller was too desperate—and no amount of money would induce them to get involved.

Chapter 3

YOU CAN'T FIRE YOUR BROTHER

Don't go into business with family, friends, or any other close acquaintances, who know you well on some other basis than business. That extends not only into partnerships as discussed in the last chapter, but into any form of business relationship. This should come as no surprise to you. Politicians are looked upon very poorly if they hire or do business with relatives or friends. Physicians and surgeons routinely refer their friends and relatives to other physicians and surgeons because their emotional involvement clouds their judgment. Attorneys can be accused of a conflict of interest if they do business with their friends or family. Your real estate investment business can suffer from the very same conflict of interest. You can't fire your brother.

Years ago in one of my first business ventures, I went into business with my brother and although the agreement said we were to be equal in all things, it soon resulted in one brother giving orders and the other brother following them. And if one is not performing according to expectations, there is no way of telling him without jeopardizing close sibling relationships. Don't go into business with friends or family.

The workings of business lend themselves to disappointments and failure on a day-to-day basis. These disappointments and failures can carry over into the family or friendship, which should be separate and distinct. These relationships are much more important and long lasting then any business deal could possibly be. These relationships are also far more rewarding than any amount of wealth or profit.

SHELTER YOUR SPOUSE

Your spouse, especially, should be sheltered from the ups and downs of your business. You don't need trouble in your home, so don't allow your spouse to be involved. If it is unavoidable, limit, by agreement, the extent and areas of involvement as much as possible. Don't share your worries and day-to-day disappointments with him/her. You may know, in the context of your broader business dealings, that a failure or problem is of minor significance, but to your spouse it may seem major and his/her feelings for you may hinge disproportionately on that temporary setback. This may prove to be my most important advice to you: shelter your spouse from your business dealings.

FRIENDS

As for friends—we recently settled a real estate transaction with a fellow, who insisted on using his attorney as a settlement attorney. It seemed all right to us at the time, but we discovered, to our dismay, that this person was not a real estate attorney. Although he may have been very competent in other areas of the law, he was bumbling and totally incompetent in the area of real estate law and practice. We found ourselves, out of necessity telling him what to do. We even had to help him calculate the figures on the balance sheets. We had to structure the deal on paper, and once the paperwork was done, he failed to process it in a timely manner. Consequently, what should have been a simple and quick settlement, extended several weeks until it was finally resolved. As a matter of fact, he bumbled so badly that he almost killed the entire transaction.

This attorney was a personal friend of the other party to the deal and had asked for the business. Because he was a friend, he was hired. Because he was a friend, he could also not be fired. You can't fire your brother, remember? It's bad business to be in business with friends.

It may happen, however, that those with whom you successfully do business may become your friends, but that is the way it should start rather than the other way around. In business first, and become friends later.

Chapter 4

BEWARE THE FRIENDLY STRANGER

Never trust your best interests to your real estate agent. No realtor, with a commission at stake in a prospective transaction, despite the best of intentions, can be an objective participant in the deal. In order to gain the more complete allegiance of your realtor, retain him as a "buyer's broker." By doing so, his split of the commissions is paid directly by you, the buyer, and not by the seller. As a fact of business, of human nature, and as a matter of law in most states, an agent's loyalty is to the person who signs his paycheck. By paying an agent $100 or so to retain him, and by guaranteeing him (his agency) the normal commission split of the sale price, you can bring him over emotionally and legally into your "camp."

Many successful investors employ a good realtor under a "buyer's broker" arrangement, or even under salary to work exclusively with them. The purpose of this action is to insure that the agent represents the investor's best interests in every case.

In one sense, though, even this precaution is futile. No third party can be aware of all your needs and wants, all the pressures and stresses you face and all the factors involved in your decision-making process. No other person knows your personal situation well enough to make choices for you. All recommendations are guesses at what they think will satisfy your needs.

It is not safe to even assume that an agent cares what happens to your interest in a transaction. I remember the day my wife and I walked into a real estate office to ask some questions about the houses in the neighborhood. One agent was watching us through the window as we walked up to the front door. As we entered, that agent bounded up to us with a big smile and said, "I love you, I love you. Come in." I thought, "It's nice to be appreciated, but this is a little strange."

In the process of her dealings with us, she sold us a house for two thousand dollars more than it was listed for and arranged financing that cost us ten times what it should have cost us. She also, in collusion with her broker, pulled several other cute tricks that would have cost her her license, had I known then what I know now about real estate practices.

You may recall what we discussed in Chapter II about choosing partners on the basis of being a "great guy." Be suspicious of anyone who wants to deal with you on the basis of an unwarranted love or respect. If he thinks you're a swell person, and that's the basis of your business transaction, step back and take another look.

I do want to stop short of saying, "Don't trust anyone in

business"—but just short of that. There are those whom you should **not** trust, however, and among them are those who exhibit an emotional response to you that is not warranted by a depth of experience. Feigning an inappropriate friendship in a business situation is just one element of the common "Con game." Don't get "conned."

Chapter 5

DON'T LET NON-RISK-TAKERS BUY AND SELL YOU

I was sitting at a settlement table figuring casually how much money everybody at the table was making on my transaction. I wasn't being cheap or envious in any way, but it occurred to me that I was the only one there who was signing a paper obligating myself to a liability. I was happy to take the risk because I had every hope of a good return on my investment, but as I counted the thousands of dollars that were being disbursed, I realized that there were a lot of people making a lot of money from my transaction, who were not involved in any risk taking. There was a six percent commission, which was split in several ways, the attorney was taking several hundred dollars for his services and the lender was taking points up front for placing the loan. On top of that, some unexpected expenses were pointed out to me. I remember thinking magnanimously, "Oh well, that's just a couple of thousand dollars less that I'm going to make when I sell the house. So what?"

My plan for this investment was to improve the house and immediately put it back on the market. The market, however, was not good at the time. Six months went by before we even got an offer on the house. The offer was considerably lower than we had anticipated. As we finalized the sale, the same feeling was still fresh in my mind that I had when we bought the house; a lot of people were making money on this project who had not taken any risks at all. In the end, after we were finally free from the property, we had lost about six thousand dollars all in less than six months. Six thousand dollars was almost, needless to say, the cost of closing the purchase and the sale. I had paid all of the non-risk takers out of pocket! Needless to say, I felt I had been taken.

Being a real estate agent myself, I don't advocate circumventing all of the middlemen. The service of a good real estate agent can be very helpful in the initial phases of your investment business, but my caution is this: Carefully consider the cost of buying, the cost of handling, and the cost of selling **before** committing to a transaction. Buying and selling the same building, depending on the commissions conventional to your area, may cost you between 10 and 15 percent of the eventual sale price of the unit. The profit margin must be much wider than that before you should even consider getting into the project.

Use middlemen to profit you in your business. Don't let non-risk-takers use you to profit them in their business.

Chapter 6

GET IT ALL IN WRITING

Sometimes a great deal of negotiating goes on between the buyer and the seller before the actual agreement is reached. Many things may be agreed to all at one time, or it may take a long time to agree on one or two items. Either situation lends itself to forgetfulness. If you haven't been writing down and initialing each point all along, you may find yourself haggling about each point all over again when it's time to sign the contract. This may be due to innocent forgetfulness, to which each of us is subject, but "forgetfulness" may also be a matter of convenience when one party has changed his or her mind and wants out of some one part of the deal, or out of the whole deal entirely.

When you are negotiating, use plenty of paper. Take a legal pad and write down every suggestion, back and forth. When agreement is reached upon a term, write it down and circle it. After all terms are dealt with in that way, have all parties initial the paper. Make copies and distribute them and then from those copies write the contract on a legal form.

Write down everything. Write down all the details of the transaction. Leave nothing to word of mouth. Nothing! Word of mouth is not, with very few exceptions, legally binding. Remember, if it's verbal, it's not an agreement.

If the other party is uncomfortable with writing it all down, suggest to him that you're writing it down for your own benefit so you don't forget. (Don't tell him it is for your benefit, so he doesn't back out of the deal and/or renege on some promises.) If anyone tells you that "his work is his bond," or "a handshake is an agreement between gentlemen," tell him, "Yes, I'm sure it is, but you don't mind if I put it in writing for my own benefit, do you?" Again, any agreements that are not in writing and signed are not agreements at all. Get it all down in writing.

WRITE DOWN EVERYTHING

Writing it down and getting signatures are also good selling tools. At the very moment that a person makes up his mind and **signs his name**, he is committed legally, and even more importantly, psychologically. If he doesn't sign his name immediately after making the decision, he can change his mind at any time, for any reason. If he has signed something, nothing can be altered without the consent of all signatory parties—he knows it, and he knows that you know it. Get him to sign something, anything. Even if it's not in legal form, psychologically he's committed. Furthermore, on the basis of written documents, you have the right to sue for performance, if need be. On the basis of a word and a handshake, you have nothing.

It would be a wonderful world if we could do business on a handshake and a gentlemen's agreement. There are those who claim to have always done business that way and are perfectly comfortable to continue doing business that way. Don't be one of them. Get it all in writing.

Chapter 7

SET THE

RECORD STRAIGHT

When you buy "on contract" you will be offering to pay the seller his equity in the property in monthly payments without refinancing the purchase through a bank. Because conveying the title or merely conveying an equitable interest in the property is grounds for the first trust lender to call non assumable loans due immediately, neither buyer nor seller will want the lender to find out about the sale. Some will suggest that you not record the contract of sale. Watch out!

When a purchase is made without having that transaction entered into the land records of the county, the buyer is in an extremely vulnerable position. Nothing, except the integrity of the seller can prevent the seller from borrowing again against the property and encumbering it with other recorded liens, which the **buyer** will have to eventually pay or lose his interest in the property.

The buyer is not only vulnerable to the acts of the seller but also vulnerable to the omissions of the seller, meaning that the Government, or any other creditor can attach liens to any property that is in the name of the seller in order to collect back taxes or other debts owed them. Even if the seller is dealing in good faith and is unaware of the back taxes or the defaulted debt, as long as that seller is the owner of record, the property can be attached. **The buyer's interest cannot be protected unless his interest is recorded.**

There are popular notions being voiced today about the conveying ownership of real estate through non-recorded instruments as being the way to buy and sell real estate. I am aware of several of those methods. Only one of them, that I know of, protects the buyer's interest as a matter of public record. Even this method does not protect the buyer fully against acts and omissions of the seller who is still the owner of record. For a more complete discussion of those instruments, see my book, *Here We Go 'Round The Due-On-Sale Claue."* In it, I explain a way to protect the seller's and the buyer's interests by public record, without disclosing all of the details of the transaction. The point is make every transaction a matter of public record.

Usually what is recorded is a contract of sale and a deed conveying title to real estate. You can also have deeds recorded conveying personal property. For that matter, you can enter into the land records of the county any sort of paper at all; leases, liens, contracts of any sort, wills, even love letters. The act of recording gives notice to all the world that an interest in a property has been conveyed. All other creditors can receive their claims against the title holder **only** after the claims of the prior lien holders are satisfied.

It is also important to remember that the order in which the claims against property are **paid** is not the order in which the debts were **incurred.** They are instead, paid in the order in which the claims were **recorded** in the public records. This means that an installment contract which is not recorded could be doing just fine, for years and years without any sign of trouble and a claim against the owner of record could at that time still be filed on the property. This new claim would be paid **prior** to the interest of the non-recorded buyer. The lienholder could even foreclose and force the sale of the building over the protests of the non-recorded buyer.

Attorneys and escrow agents and others, who are sworn to uphold the public interest, can function in a similar way by storing documents for safe keeping. Any time there is a question about the status of the property, the documents are accessible for reference purposes, but the full protection of recordation is not there.

Protect yourself by making your interest in a property a matter of public record.

Chapter 8

HUMANOIDS

I'm a reasonable fellow. If you make a commitment to me of any sort and can't meet your commitment because of some circunstances that are beyond your control, I'd understand. At such a time, we would do the best we could to work it out together.

I went into real estate with the same feeling. When it comes to lending money secured by real estate, the law says that a lender can foreclose if necessary. "Of course foreclosure can happen," I thought, "but not to me. The lender is a reasonable person. My intentions are honorable, and certainly a reasonable person would not foreclose on another person, who honorably intends to meet his commitments."

That sadly warped perspective of the business world only lasted through my first investment transaction. It was then I discovered that lenders are not people. Lenders are humanoids; machines, if you will. They process people and spit out money. They don't "understand" when you have trouble meeting your commitments. Your lack of meeting a commitment is merely one more opportunity to take money from you as a penalty. And if your problems are sufficiently severe, the law entitles them to take your property from you and sell it to distribute your equity amongst attorneys, the courts, collection agencies, other agents and themselves.

The lenders have structured their loans such that their exposure, their possibility of loss in the case of foreclosure, is minimal. They will loan only up to what they think your house will bring at an auction, generally 80%. If they need to, they can sell your property at auction, take their money and move on. In other words they arrange it so the risk is all the borrower's and not the lender's.

Their "understanding" of borrower's troubles stops at the upper limit of their maximum exposure, not one dollar more. That upper exposure limit includes the time it takes to go to court to foreclose and resell the property at auction to get their money back, not one day longer. So, if you happen to be a day late or a dollar short, due to some reason beyond your control, what you can expect from your lender is that the process of seizing and selling your home has already begun.

FORECLOSURE

I remember thinking, "Foreclosure only happens to people who refuse to make their payments; bums, drug addicts and crooks." I discovered that it also happens to widows, people whose only crime is forgetfulness or care-lessness, people who are the victims of bad luck, people who lose their jobs because their companies go out of business, or people who can't work because they're too sick. I remember thinking that it couldn't happen to me. But it can and it did.

With one of my properties, my plan to sell had not materialized, so I asked the lender to renew the loan or extend its term, thinking surely it would be to his advan-tage to not have to place that money again. The interest rate I was paying was above market and profitable to him. Even after I explained all the legitimate problems I'd encountered along with the reasons why he should extend, his response was to promptly begin foreclosure proceed-ings. I thought to myself, "This can't really be happening to me. I'm not refusing to make my payments. I'm not a bum, a drug addict, or a crook." I called him several times to tell him so, but he simply said, "Tell it to my attorney."

Finally, the day before my property was to be sold to the highest bidder on the steps of the county courthouse, his attorney called me and said that the lender had had second thoughts, and had decided to extend the term. I thought, "See! He is a reasonable person after all." "But," his law-yer continued, "only if you immediately pay another $1,500 plus all the back interest owed, and $900 for legal fees. Then he will extend it, but only for another 90 days."

It occurred to me that his magnanimity may have resulted from his doubt that the property in its present condition, would bring enough at auction to pay off the loan he had made to us. Also, the prospects of collecting a deficiency judgment (see Chapter 26) out of state were not good. Offering it back to us at the last moment before the gavel fell was a shrewd method of encumbering the property further, so that he and his attorney could foreclose on it again 90 days later. They were milking us dry.

With these thoughts in mind, I was an angry man as I walked into that attorney's office to sign the papers allowing us to extend the loan. I believe the attorney actually expected me to thank him for offering this last minute reconciliation. If the lender was able to extend now, why wasn't he able to 30 days ago, before socking us with $900 of fees to his lawyer? I didn't thank him.

This situation is hopefully not typical of what your investment experience will be, but it is typical of what the lenders **can** do upon default. It **can** happen to you.

WORK IT OUT

Something might well be said here about the ripple theory. At the point of contact with the surface of the lake, a stone makes a relatively small disturbance. But the longer you wait, the larger the circle of waves gets. If you are at odds in any way with your lender, **go to him immediately and work it out.** If you can't make a payment this month, tell him. The earlier, the better. You might even go to him **before** the payment is due to inform him it will be late. He will be more favorably disposed towards allowing you to work it out, if you get to him before he has to call you asking where the payment is. If he will not allow you to work it out (presume this to begin with), at the very least you know early-on what his intentions are. His disposition will only get worse, like the ripples in the lake, the longer you wait to tell him the bad news.

I have a tendency to ignore the bad news, hoping that it will go away. I think maybe I'll win the sweepstakes in time to make the payment, or something. But bad news is like a toothache—it only gets worse.

Whatever you do, don't expect understanding from lenders.

Chapter 9

CHECK OUT EVERYTHING FOR YOURSELF

In my business as a realtor, I was somewhat amused to watch across the settlement table as some other agent would run through the settlement sheets the attorney had prepared, checking all the figures for totals and subtotals. I thought to myself, "It's the attorney's job to be exact and precise in all things." Well, not long ago, I realized the value of checking everything for yourself.

I borrowed money secured by a second trust on a property of mine. It was agreed that I would borrow $15,000 for two years, at 18% interest, payable in monthly installments of interest only. When we got to the settlement table to sign the papers and get the loan; the note read: $15,000 at 18%, simple interest, payable interest only, in monthly installments of $250. The entire amount, $15,000, to be due and payable 24 months from date of settlement. I thought, "That's our agreement, I'll sign the papers." When it came time, 24 months later, to pay the balloon, I got out the papers to find out the exact due date. Just on a whim, I got out my calculator and ran through the figures. Eighteen percent of $15,000 paid monthly came to exactly $225 per month. I rechecked the figures and they were correct. I had been paying $250 all along thinking that I was paying interest only. Obviously, $25 of my payment should be deducted monthly from the principal, reducing the balance owed.

I called the lender to ask him what the exact payoff figure would be. His response was, "You agreed to pay $250, and pay me $15,000 at the end of the term. That is what the payoff figure is." Expecting that he had misunderstood, and also expecting that he was a reasonable person (big mistake, see Chapter 7), I carefully explained to him again how a mistake had been made on the face of the note, and that I had actually been paying $25 more per month than the simple interest-only payments that we had agreed upon. I was surprised to hear him say, "You owe me $15,000. That's it." It finally dawned on me that he had no intention of reconciling this error with the original agreement that we had entered into.

CHECK EVERYTHING OUT

It would have been a very simple thing to have taken my calculator to the settlement table two years prior, and have quickly run through the figures. No one would have taken any offense at doing it, and that very simple act of checking it out for myself would have saved me several hundred dollars over a two year period, plus all the aggravation of dealing with a lender who saw and seized upon an opportunity for gain by getting more than what was due him.

Check out everything for yourself. Any claims of any party in a business transaction should be checked out. Again, I don't want to say, "Don't trust anybody in business," but perhaps something close to that.

The county courthouse and the county land records are wonderful tools to get the information you need, and the public servants who work there are very willing to answer any of your questions and to tell you how to find any specific information you may need.

As a real estate sales agent, I was very amused one time while working with a first-time buyer. He would ask me for certain information and I would tell him, "I can get that information for you and I'll let you know later." When I called the city or county offices to ask, I was told that someone had called just moments before, asking for that exact same information. This happened repeatedly over the course of several days and I had to laugh when I discovered that my customer was doing his own homework and checking everything out for himself.

You might be surprised at all the information that is available over the phone from people who are paid just to answer your questions. It is information available to anyone who just asks for it.

Chapter 10

STIFLE !

How many stories can you tell of persons who spent years carefully building toward a goal, attentive to every detail, planning and precisely executing each plan, who finally succumbed to an impulse, and watched the fruits of years of work fall to pieces through the effects of that one impulsive action. It has happened in every field of endeavor: Every art, science, business, or adventure. It has happened in every age and in every civilization of man. Literature of every tongue tells the same story in simple terms and complex plots as fables (The Tortois and the Hare) and as documentary history (King David in the Bible).

The age-old counsel is: Easy does it, slow and steady. The world belongs to the plodders who walk a straight course and endure to the end. Despite all this evidence and testimony, we still jump to our impulses and seek the quick and easy path to "success." Certainly there are a few who "make it" quick and easy by following an impulse. But impulses are so often wrong that there must be thousands who lose for every one who wins on an impulse. Because we only hear the "success" stories of the "overnight wonders" and never the stories of the thousands who lose, we tend to think that the odds are in favor of success, when actually they are heavily weighted against impulsiveness.

I was told recently about an investor who, over ten years, carefully built a substantial real estate empire in Denver. He always checked things out completely, and studiously avoided the more speculative projects. One evening at a party, an acquaintance mentioned a deal in which he could double a $10,000 investment in three weeks. Although it involved drugs, this careful man on an impulse, decided that a three week vulnerability was worth the reward. He joined the venture. The deal was busted, he was arrested and spent a year in prison, during which time he lost his empire. He lost everything he had worked for for ten years. When he was released, he was not just starting over, he was a convicted felon starting over. He let an impulse get by unchecked.

FOLLOWING IMPULSES

We need to catch ourselves as we begin to yield to an impulse. Since our natural tendencies cannot be depended on at that instant, an artificial system can be helpful. A checklist of sorts. Airline pilots have a list of items to check each and everytime they prepare for a takeoff. They may use that list thousands of times during their careers, and they may have it memorized, but they are required to go down the list item by item none-the-less. This is an artificial system to curb the impulse to takeoff unprepared.

Many of us have taken off unprepared in real estate for lack of a checklist. Some investors have developed their own criteria for investing (see Chapter 16). These criteria are only a superimposed checklist to prevent impulsive actions. As you gain experience, you should devise your own checklist to go through in evaluating a prospective transaction—your own investment criteria. My forthcoming book, *The Smart Start Handbook,* may be helpful as you devise your own system of checks.

Some suggestions as you begin your investment business:

1. Check with your accountant. What will the net effect of this transaction be on your financial picture? **Do you really need it?**

2. If your proposed deal is legally questionable, or if it is creative beyond the scope of your experience, check with an attorney. **Is it legal?**

Before you step to another stratum of property type, from single family to multi-unit, from multi-unit to hotel, from duplex to office building, speak with 10 owners and 10 managers of that type of property to learn what to look out for, and what troubles to expect. **Do you really want to do it?**

4. Before stepping into a new market area, or a new property type, maybe before finalizing any deal, get an appraisal of its current value by an uninvolved third party; someone other than your agent. **Is it really worth this much?**

5. If an unfamiliar property type is involved, get a structural and systems inspection. You can do your own on single family or duplex types if you know what you are looking for. But remember, different rules (codes) apply to different types of buildings. **Will this building eat you up in repairs?**

6. Check specifically for building code compliance. In Virginia, for example, you can operate a not-up-to-code system (plumbing, electrical, etc.) and mend existing components, but any change or upgrading or addition of new components, requires the **entire** system to be brought up to code. A planned $600 improvement to a kitchen and a certain quick profit could end up being a $6,000 renovation and a loss when code violations come into play. You'd better know before you go. **Worry about the codes.**

The profits will come in real estate as the mistakes are avoided. Spend more time evaluating risks rather than counting promises. **Check your impulsiveness. Everytime.**

Chapter 11

MAKE YOUR MONEY WHEN YOU BUY, NOT WHEN YOU SELL

It's fallacious to think that, because you are reaping the reward of your investment when you sell, that those rewards are generated at the time of sale. Not so. Those rewards are generated by your ownership of the property, how you have improved it and by market forces at work over the term of your ownership. That term of ownership started when you bought the property. Most of the conditions that governed your ownership were established by you when you purchased the property. Most notably in times when the real estate market is slow (a "buyer's market"), but also in times of good sales volume, **buyers** dictate the terms of the sale to a greater extent than do the sellers.

As I was listing houses as part of my realty business, I

had to keep reminding the sellers that the actual value of a house can only be established by what someone is willing to pay for it at any particular time. It is not established by what the sellers think it's worth, but what someone is actually willing to pay them for it. Demand is what creates value, and demand is controlled by **buyers**. Only the supply is controlled by sellers. In any given transaction, then, the buyer determines for himself what he will pay for the property, plus the other terms of the sale, not the seller. The point here is that you make money when you are in control, and you are in control when you buy—not when you sell.

On the other hand, you will not be able to buy unless the seller is willing to sell. So it is of great importance to discover the dominant need of the seller. The dominant need may be to get a certain amount of cash out of the transaction, regardless of the terms under which he disposes of the balance of his equity. On the other hand, because of taxation, it might be advantageous to the seller to take installment payments instead of cash. The investor needs to be skillful in explaining those advantages to the seller. Of course the less amount of the investor's own money involved, the more advantageous for him.

SELLER'S NEEDS

You can very often discover the seller's needs by simply asking why he needs a certain amount of cash or what he intends to do with it. If he intends to pay off liens on the property those liens might be assumed by the buyer, thereby cutting back on the amount of cash brought by the buyer into the transaction. Many lenders are approachable on this subject if more favorable terms are offered to them by the prospective buyer. If the cash is to be used by the seller in another investment, the effective return of that investment might be matched by the terms of the note that the seller is to take back. If the seller needs the cash to purchase another home or make another large purchase, you may suggest that he make that next purchase on installments, or under other terms that will not require the cash that he was planning to put out.

If there's an agent representing the seller in the transaction, that agent's cash needs in terms of commissions have a direct bearing on the seller's cash needs. In the interest of putting together and keeping together a transaction, the listing agent could very well be convinced that taking his commission in some other form than cash, like a small note on the property conveyed, or another commodity, could be to his advantage. As a realtor, I put together one sale involving investment grade gems. I asked the listing agent to consider taking her commission in gems, describing the advantages of this type of investment for her purposes. She agreed to do it which facilitated my buyer getting into the transaction with very little cash.

One other suggestion regarding cash needs. If you have an agent representing you, the buyer, that agent also has some cash needs that will dictate the cash you must bring into the transaction. As a former realtor, I still have loyalty to the real estate profession, so I don't want to suggest that cutting out the middle man is the thing to do. But if only one agency is involved in the transaction, representing both buyer and seller, commission monies may be cut in half. The resulting commissions would be exactly equal to what the listing agency would have received if another agency had bought your contract and your cash going into the deal would be much less.

Let me illustrate. Where I sold real estate, the commission for selling a house is 6%. That 6% is split between the listing agency, who represents the seller, and the selling agency, who represents the buyer, each receiving 3%. If an investor sees a house that is listed by a particular agent, and goes directly to that agent, offering a transaction that gives that agency 3%, exactly the same amount of money as if another agency had bought the transaction, in the interest of earning that commission immediately, the listing agent would probably cooperate. By doing this, the investor cuts 3% off the sales price of the house, and also a great deal of cash from the immediate cash requirements of the seller.

Another important consideration about making your money when you buy, not when you sell, is monthly payments. If your investment strategy is to buy the property and rent it out for a period of time, monthly cash flow becomes a very important concern, more important even than the purchase price of the property. Very often, the seller will take less money per month on his terms if the full listing price is offered. Even offering more than the listing price for the house is a very good inducement to the seller for taking less on a monthly basis.

There are many types of financing available now from conventional lenders. Those types of financing can be applied to financing the seller's equity in such a way that very low monthly payments are made. Zero interest loans, rapid repayment loans, adjustable rate loans, graduated payment loans, and other forms of financing are simply tools that can help you to structure the purchase of a seller's equity and bring down your monthly payments. My book, **The Great Mortgage Money Mystery**, may be very helpful to you for learning those alternative financing types and in turn, help you structure a transaction for your investment purposes.

Chapter 12

DUCKS IN A ROW, THEN GO

A realtor is trained to assist the purchaser to make a quick firm commitment to the property and to the transaction. One of my buyers was an investor-builder. He·was very deliberate in the things he did. He was so ponderous, that it became particularly frustrating for me, a well trained realtor, to wait for him to make his decisions.

The proposal in question involved renovating a building after applying for and obtaining certain variances from the county. This man refused to make any move at all without having everything checked out and arranged first. He was going well beyond what we discussed in chapter 9. When he was finally prepared to act, he offered only a contingent contract, demanding that all approvals be given before any monies convey. This is apparently commonplace with large commercial property dealings, but I was not prepared for it in residential sales.

For six months, while the county was grinding through

its processes, the entire transaction was in limbo. The property was tied up but none of the investor's money was tied up or in jeopardy of being lost. No one knew if we had a sale or not. I was going crazy and the sellers were going crazy. Everything was to the advantage of the investor and it stayed that way.

I learned a little something about investment from this rather extreme example; put your ducks in a row before you go. This is diametrically opposite from what I was trained to do in residential sales. It also seems opposite from what is advised in many of the investment books on the market today. The impression is often given that you should "paint with a broad brush" and let the "details" resolve themselves.

LOSING IS NO FUN!

I recall from the first book I read on real estate investment (the same one which motivated me so greatly to get into the market) the impression that tying up the property and buying it were of primary concern. How you paid for it was only of secondary importance. All that would just work out somehow. I entered into several deals with this attitude and soon found that there are a lot of ways to lose money. Incidentally, I also found that my threshold of pain, in terms of losing money on a real estate transaction is extremely low. I had to ask myself, "So, what's so great about losing money?" The answer is "Nothing." Losing money is no fun at all.

I firmly believe at this point, that there is no reason to lose money in real estate. Every transaction can be structured so that losing on the deal is virtually impossible. It may take months of searching before you find a property that you can handle without risk, but my feeling now is that if the deal is not exactly right for your purposes, stay away from it.

When you're buying a home to live in, gain and loss do not figure into your transaction quite as heavily, because there is significant value in your use of the property while you are living in it. Since living in it generally dictates a longer period of ownership than is necessary as an investor to reap your profits, due to appreciation over the long term, loss is not even a real possibility.

What you absolutely do not want to do as an investor is hurry into a deal, especially into your first three or four or five. Once you get a little further down the road, you can have some of your better investments absorb any temporary negative cash flows or temporary set backs of other investments. At that time, your experience will allow you to make better decisions a lot faster than before. So your most crucial purchases are your first several which will get you established in the business of real estate investments. **Get your ducks in a row, then go.**

Some investors are so adept at this particular concept of planning every detail in advance, that they can literally sell the property before they own it. I've always thought that to be the ideal arrangement; acting as a middleman and minimizing their own risk and liability in the transaction.

Let's talk about some ducks for a moment, and then

we'll talk about how to get them in a row. There's a wealth of information available over the telephone from the city or county records. For instance, by simply asking, you can get the name and mailing address of the owner of any property in the county. You can get a legal description, the zoning regulations and what's applicable on that specific property, as well as the likelihood of change by the Zoning Commission. You can get an appraised value, divided into the values for the land and for the improvements, and you can find out what taxes are paid on the property. You can find from the land records if there are any liens on the property, easements and dedications given against the land, and of course, who is the legal owner and how title is being held.

REAL ESTATE AGENCIES

Real estate agencies are a great source of information that can be very valuable to an investor. Any listing agent will be happy to give you all the information he can possibly find about his own listing, including, from the facts immediately available to him, the legal description of the land parcel, the latest previous purchase price, of that property and many other details of that prior transaction including comparable properties that have sold in the neighborhood to help you establish an offering price. They can also give you a list of other units of the same type available for purchase. Many real estate offices also deal in rentals and can give you current rental values for that type of property and vacancy rates in the immediate area. Any agency can give you a list of expected closing costs. They have forms called "Net sheets" (one for the buyer and one for the seller) that can be used to figure out what the closing costs will be for each party. You can use these net sheets to structure your offer to the seller, showing him what his bottom line take home cash will be. You can also get contract forms from the agencies to use in your transactions—forms that have already been approved for use in your state.

LENDERS

Call the lenders. They can give you a lot of information on what financing is available for that particular property in the way of purchase money or for renovation loans. It is conceivable that the property, if it is in poor condition, is not even lendable according to their criteria. They can give you qualifying information as to the maximum amounts they will loan you based on the value of the property and your income structure.

STRUCTURAL INSPECTION

A structural inspection can be helpful when the property is of doubtful structural integrity. However, it can also be expensive and ineffective in helping you make the decisions you need to make. You might like to use my forth-coming book, **A TEN MINUTE STRUCTURAL INSPECTION** for an inexpensive way to put that particular duck in a row.

One very important thing to consider here is that while you are busy getting your ducks in a row, the property may well be sold to another investor who can make his decisions more quickly. If that happens, remember that one deal will not make or break your career. You may lose several deals, but it is better to lose a few when there are more just like it coming onto the market everyday, than to hurry into something that will eventually hurt you.

TYING UP PROPERTY

One rule of thumb is never tie up in a project more money in earnest money or costs of any kind, than you are prepared to walk away from and lose completely.

There are ways that you can tie up a property without losing one dollar if you need to drop it. While you are putting your ducks in a row, you can keep the property from being sold to another person in any of several ways. One method is the purchase of an option.

You purchase the option to buy (at a later date) from the seller by giving him a certain amount of money. This purchase option may take the form of a "right of first refusal," which means that you have the right, over the term of your option, to match any bona-fide offer to purchase that is brought to the seller. In this way, the seller continues to market his property and when the first offer is brought in, you have the opportunity to match that offer.

Another type of option allows the purchaser of the option the right, for a certain length of time, to buy the property at a set price under predetermined terms. The purchaser of the option also has the right not to buy it at all, in which case, generally, the option price is forfeited. Many investors make a lot of money by simply buying options and selling them (the options) to other investors, who want to consummate the transaction under those terms. This is one form of selling the property before you own it.

One other, and probably the simplest form of tying up the property without committing to it unwisely, is the use of contingencies in the sale contract. The purchaser, who has some ducks to put in a row before he concludes the deal, will allow himself several escape clauses in the sales agreement. These are contingencies written into the purchase proposal such as: "contract contingent upon (or subject to...) Aunt Ethel's approval" or "...upon satisfactory structural inspection..." or upon anything at all that the purchaser wants to write in. It is well known among real estate agents that a contract that has this kind of contingency is worth absolutely nothing until those contingencies are withdrawn in writing. In other words, the purchaser has the right to withdraw the contract and reclaim his earnest money deposit if those contingencies are not satisfied. And most contingencies, though written to indicate otherwise, depend solely upon the purchaser's continued desire to stay in the deal and nothing more.

CONTINGENT CONTRACT

The effect of even a contingent contract on a house is that all other contracts that may come in have to wait for approval by the seller until the contingencies in the first contract are either removed or the first contract is withdrawn.

A word to sellers: Accept a contract with any contingencies ONLY with a 72 hour "kick out" clause. This protection should be worded similarly to this: "The purchaser agrees to remove the contingencies or withdraw the contract within 72 hours of written notification from the seller to do so." I have seen purchasers tie up a property with contingencies and refuse to release it for many months. There was no "kick out" clause, and the seller finally had to go to court in order to sell the property to someone else.

A word to buyers: When a contract is "working" on a house, the tendency is to "lay off" and look elsewhere. Don't pass up a tremendous bargain that way. The house is not **sold** until all parties have signed the contract and initialed all its changes. You or your agent can register a contract with the listing agency and demand to present it immediately, if not sooner even if there is a contract on the property already. It is common for several contracts to be presented at the same sitting with the seller. The best deal for the seller wins. Even if the contract is in counter or recounter phase, until **all** terms are agreed to and signed, the house is **not sold**. It is still available to any buyer. The listing agency is required, in the interest of the seller, to allow any contract that is registered with them to be presented. The listing agency may not like it, especially if the other contract is through an "in house" agent, but that is the law.

The best policy, then, is to immediately attempt to tie up the property with a contingent contract, or an option agreement of some sort, and then go back, put your ducks in a row. If they don't go in a row, bail out of the deal by exercising your contingency. When the ducks finally are in a row, then go ahead with the transaction.

Chapter 13

BUY NOW, PAY LATER

I don't know where, as I started my investment career, that I got the impression that in order to capitalize on the really good deals, I would have to move so fast that I'd be making the big moves and let the details work themselves out as I go. how that translated right away into my business was "Buy it now, quick, before it gets away—figure out how to pay for it later." Obviously, I hadn't read chapter 12 of this book yet. I began living on margin and the margin was all eventually nibbled out from under me.

The part of each person's income which is left after all the legal or contractual obligations are fulfilled, after the mortgage payment, utilities, car payments and such are paid, is called "discretionary income." When I made my first investment and agreed to what became a constant negative cash flow, I had committed a good part of my discretionary income. What I didn't realize was that that money was no longer discretionary. Maybe I thought that if I ran out of money, I just wouldn't make that one payment, and everybody would understand. I obviously hadn't read chapter 8 of this book yet, either. Once discretionary income is committed to a legal obligation, it is no longer discretionary income. That is the danger in any kind of negative cash flow.

One investor I knew had been committing all of his discretionary income for so long, that although his holdings totaled close to a million dollars, he lived in an old house, which had not been renovated and his family wore old clothes and drove an old car. Because the kitchen plumbing was in such chronically poor condition, his wife washed their dishes in the bathtub, for over a year. It occurred to me that discretionary income which is applied to food and clothing and providing for yourself a standard of living, is probably the least discretionary income of all.

The reason you're investing to begin with is to provide a standard of living for yourself. If, because of your investments, your standard of living goes down, then you have forgotten the goal of your investment career.

BALLOON PAYMENTS

One other form of buying now and paying later is what is called "balloon" payments; large payments of principal only that are due in a big chunk at a later date. I believe it is wise counsel not to get involved in balloon payments. The reason is that each of us has very little control over the economic conditions that govern our investing. Many times, how much money we make, or how much money we are able to save, or how much money we are able to borrow, are functions of market conditions which are beyond our control.

How can anyone promise that two years down the line one's personal financial positions and the general market will be such that the required balloon payments will be able to be borrowed or saved? And although your payment record may be spotless, with all payments on time and all accounts current, you can still be foreclosed upon and lose your house or investment because you can't make a balloon payment. The counsel is to **avoid balloon payments.**

If you plan on a negative cash flow, set aside discretionary income to begin with so that you are not being cannibalized by your investments and forced to live in poverty.

Chapter 14

HOW DO YOU DEDUCT
FROM NOTHING

Because of the tax structure in the United States, one of the most persuasive reasons for investing in real estate is that you can recapture your tax dollars. It is true. There are tremendous tax advantages to owning investment property, but those tax breaks are only an advantage to you personally up to a point. Beyond that, they are not an advantage at all. This may sound very simple and obvious, but how many people run into trouble because they forget this very point?

Everyone realizes that you could lose money in rental property through, for instance, a negative cash flow. But the standard reply is, "Isn't it great? It's all deductible! You get it all back!" I even felt at one time that there was some perverse advantage to losing money. I have to look back now and laugh at myself during my first few investments. I was thinking of the tremendous tax breaks of owning rental property, but at the end of the year it was apparent that I had no income to deduct from. It finally dawned on me that you can't "get it all back" if you never had it to begin with.

BLESS THE BANK

One of the first goals we should be striving for in our investment careers is to get to the point where we are paying no taxes because all our tax deductions equal our taxable income and the net result is zero tax owed.

Remember this simple equation:

$$DX + NOL + ZTB = GAI$$

The sum of all DEDUCTIBLE EXPENSES, plus the NET OPERATING LOSS on your rental units, plus the maximum ZERO TAX BRACKET income for you, EQUALS your GROSS ANNUAL INCOME.

If you are a single tax payer, filing singly, your 1982 ZTB maximum income is $2,300. If married, filing jointly, your 1982 ZTB maximum income is $3,400. In 1983 and subsequent years, those figures will change slightly due to tax cuts.

If the sum of your deductions plus your net operating loss is greater than your gross annual income above your zero tax bracket maximum, you are deducting from something that you don't have. Probably at that point, what negative cash flow you have and your actual losses are cannibalizing your discretionary income. You could be in trouble.

My suggestion to the beginning real estate investor is to set a goal to create a net operating loss only large enough so when it is added to all other deductible items and your zero tax bracket maximum, it equals your gross annual income. Once you have accomplished that goal, stop investing long enough to reassess why you are investing to begin with. If you've brought yourself to zero taxes, unless your gross income increases, don't invest any more. The danger, once again, is that your negative cash flows and the expenses of maintaining the properties will eat away at your discretionary income and instead of serving you, your investments will be hurting you.

You may, at this point, while maintaining your zero tax bracket, want to change strategies. You may want to become more speculative by buying, improving and selling houses for a profit, looking only toward cash flow and year-end income. Avoid doing what I did in my early years—building up such a great empire that you don't have the cash flow to maintain it. That is a very unhappy situation.

Your target figure is the maximum allowable income for your zero tax bracket, the ZTB in the equation. You will want to acquire tax deductions which, when subtracted from your gross annual income (GAI) will bring your income to that figure. You don't want to go to zero income or less.

On the other hand, of course, it's important to remember that the net operating losses (this paper business loss), can be extended into subsequent years; as far as 15 years from the present tax year.

Chapter 15

THE LONG COST
OF SHORT MONEY

It may not occur to the beginning investor that a 16% long term loan and a 16% short term loan do not have the same interest rate. Everytime a loan is settled, in other words, any time a loan is made and the funds are disbursed, there are certain fees paid to the people responsible for disbursing it. There are costs for preparing and recording the documents, plus Loan Origination Fees, or Loan Placement Fees. This is money paid to the lending institution or to the lending agent for his or her work in placing the loan and processing the application paperwork. These LOF's are reckoned in terms of "points." One point is one percent of the loan amount.

Incidentally, early on in my investing history, I was closing a loan in Virginia, and the lender happened to be from the District of Columbia. I was told at the loan closing that one point in the District of Columbia meant **ten** percent! Of course it doesn't. One point is one percent, that's all. I'll tell you more about that exciting story in the next chapter.

POINTS AND COSTS

The point here is that there are fees associated with placing a loan each and every time a loan is placed. Periodically some of those same points and costs may be charged again, even if the original loan is just extended for another term. How often points may be charged on the same loan is a matter of law in each state. Check your code.

In our example, a 16% long term loan has LOF's associated with it once, and then the loan, over a period of years, is paid off or amortized. A 16% short term loan has LOF's also, which, when amortized over the short term of the loan, actually increase the effective interest rate that's being paid. A 16% loan for a 12 month term, with 2 points associated with it in loan placement, is actually an 18% loan.

INTEREST RATES GO UP

One project that I had was to be a three month project. We bought the house, planning to immediately fix it up cosmetically and put it back on the market and sell it. We therefore arranged for six month financing. We figured that we had a pretty good margin, and by a week or two after settlement we would have a lot of the work done, immediately put a sign out and sell it by the time the loan was due in six months. Just after we bought it one of the agents involved said very casually, "Oh, did you hear? Today the interest rates went up." That was 1980, and we had the wonderful experience of watching all the buyers in the market drop out as the interest rate went from less than 10% to 18% over a period of six months. We couldn't sell our house.

At the end of six months, the money came due and we had to refinance but at a much higher rate, and we had to pay points again. Finally, we sold the house at $16,000 more than we paid for it, but not before suffering a significant loss. The reason? We got stuck paying the long cost of short money, not only once, but twice over the term of this investment. When I sat back and calculated it, I discovered that we had paid in the cost of financing alone, $900 per month for the months that we owned the property. That was the loan cost of short money.

The lenders loved us and the real estate agents loved us, but we didn't love them, and we didn't even like ourselves at the end of it all. We would have been much better off getting long term financing on that loan and then paying it off early. There are generally no prepayment penalties, but even if there are, they probably would be less expensive than the cost of obtaining another loan.

The net effective interest rate of any loan can be calculated very easily as follows: Take the cost of the loan (placement points, legal fees and all other costs) and divide that total by the number of months in the term of the loan.

Add that figure to the monthly interest in dollars paid on the loan. This figure represents the cost of the loan per month. Multiply that by twelve and divide that figure by the actual amount of money disbursed to you. For example:

Loan Amount	$15,000
Interest Rate	18%
Closing Costs (includes 2 pts.)	$492.00
Total Disbursed	$14,608
Net effective I.R.	18.59%
30 yrs. 15 yrs.	18.71%
1 yr.	21.85%
6 months	25.22%
3 months	31.96%

You might not think that adding a point or two would make much difference, but it does. The shorter the term of the loan, the more dramatic the influence of those points on the interest rate. Don't get caught paying the long cost of short money.

When you are considering entering into a transaction, translate every expense expressed in "points" or percentages back into dollars and cents. You don't pay your rent with percentages and you don't take your profit in points. It is easier to make a 3% mistake than a $1,537.89 mistake.

Chapter 16

TAKE A HIKE!

Don't be afraid to walk away from the settlement table. In the State of Virginia, as in other states, the purchase of real estate is formalized and concluded in the office of an attorney. It is the attorney's job to represent the contract, to be sure that all terms of the contract are fulfilled, that the paper work is properly done and that all documents are properly recorded. By the time the contract reaches the attorney prior to this settlement, all terms have been negotiated and agreed upon by both parties. And if those parties have read chapter 6 of this book they have every detail of the deal down in writing.

It frequently happens though, that at the time of settlement, when all the parties sit down to disburse funds, all of those details have not been performed according to the written contract. What do you do then?

Since "time is of the essence" of the contract, at that point, technically, you have a voidable contract. In other words, the party, whose expectations or contractual demands have not been fulfilled, has the right to void the contract and back out of the deal. That party doesn't have to, but he has the right to do so if he chooses. This could be a very important distinction to make, especially if the nature of the transaction has changed from when it was originally proposed.

If it starts to look like a bad deal, then any detail on which the other party does not perform as written, can be just cause for backing out of the deal legally. The following is a good example: The purchasers had agreed to buy the house, and as in all standard real estate contracts there is a paragraph wherein all listed personal property, or chattels, not fixed to the structure or the land, are to convey with the property. They had written in things like stove, refrigerator, existing storm windows, etc. A short time after they had bound themselves to this contract, their plans changed rather dramatically, and they no longer wanted to follow through with the purchase, but they were bound. There was no way out.

They had arranged a walk-through inspection prior to settlement, and discovered to their outward dismay, but to their inward joy, that the seller had taken out the refrigerator that was there when they wrote the contract, and had replaced it with another one. When they pointed it out to the agents involved, the seller promised to replace it with a brand new, top of the line, frost-free, automatic ice cube making, ice water dispensing refrigerator. That certainly would have appeased them except that the buyers really wanted to be out of the contract. They refused to accept the new refrigerator, voided the contract and walked away with their entire earnest money deposit. They were acting entirely within their legal rights.

VOIDABLE CONTRACTS

The point here that needs to be understood is that if some change in the transaction becomes apparent subsequent to the writing and signing of the contract, no matter what the change, no matter how insignificant or how major, even if it is as late as at the settlement table when the money is being disbursed, the contract is immediately voidable and the parties can walk away from the deal, suffering absolutely no loss.

We personally had a traumatic experience with this very point. The agent, who helped us purchase a home, also arranged for us the financing at a certain interest rate with one point. We had shopped around ourselves and the cheapest money we could find was three points, so we told her to get that loan, and we'd see her at settlement. At the settlement table the lender had already deducted 10% from the face value of the loan. The attorney said,"There must be some mistake here. We'll go into the other room and call the lender."

The attorney went into the other room accompanied by the agent and the broker and we sat there amicably chatting with the sellers across the table. In the other room they must have drawn lots to see who would tell us the bad news. They said the lender maintained that in the District of Columbia, where the lender was situated, one point meant 10%! I thought, "That's preposterous." And furthermore, that extra 9% cut significantly into the profit we had planned to make on this transaction. So there we sat, looking at the agents, the brokers, the attorney and the sellers, and they all sat there looking at us. We had a decision to make.

We had arranged through a decorator's agreement with the seller to have early access to the property to make cosmetic changes. We had already been in the house for several weeks and had spent about $1,200 in materials and labor, replacing gutters, installing a skylight, refinishing the hardwood floors, plus painting, papering and cleaning. We could walk away from all that or we could take the gamble.

Thinking, "Oh well, that's just a thousand dollars less that we're going to make on the deal," we went ahead with it. Big mistake. Due to a combination of elements, many of which were well beyond our control, we lost a lot of sleep, a lot of time and about $6,000.

A lot of things could have been done differently. What we definitely should not have done was stayed there at that settlement table. We could have protected our investment to that point by merely postponing the settlement by a week. The seller would have agreed to it, the agents would have had no choice but to agree to it. It's fairly routine, also, for attorneys to reschedule settlements and to rewrite settlement sheets. The pressure was on us, however, and we yielded to it.

Don't be afraid to walk away from the settlement table. You have the right to do it if you discover anything different from the terms that you dictated in the written document of purchase or sale.

Chapter 17

IF YOU LOVE IT,

LEAVE IT

One of the principal differences between buying a home for yourself to live in and buying for investment purposes is the emotional investment that you make in your own residence. Real estate agents are told all the time that the purchase of a home is an emotional decision. It is when buying a residence, you fall in love with a home that you want to live in and you do whatever you have to do to acquire it. The decision to purchase an investment property cannot be made that way.

A friend of mine, who puts together syndicates to purchase large commercial properties, told me recently that his company reviews 50 proposals, 50 properties for sale, every week. He personally reviews each deal that comes to his office. He immediately rejects an average of 48 of the fifty, because they don't meet the criteria he has established for his investors. He doesn't see the properties, he doesn't even know where the projects are, but he routinely rejects 96% of the proposals that he sees. He only goes to look at two of the 50 that come through his office each week. Based on that inspection, he will reject one of those two, and order an engineering and feasibility for the other. On only one of two properties which make it as far as the feasibility study, does he make a purchase proposal. His proposal to purchase is only on his terms. If that one in one hundred proposal is rejected, or it otherwise can't be brought to settlement, he says in effect, "Oh well.." and he begins looking at next week's fifty.

That is about as far from the emotional aspect of a home purchase as it could possibly get.

WORLD OF BUSINESS

The moment that you determine in your mind to purchase an investment property, you have left the realm of residential home purchasing and entered the world of business. You are a business person, and if you want to stay in business, you must conduct yourself in a detached, unemotional business-like manner. Your decisions must be based upon your investment criteria only. If you see a property that you fall in love with, leave it. Decisions that are based on emotion will not be profitable in terms of your investment goals. **If you love it, leave it.**

Sometimes I romanticize in my mind and picture each house as having a character, a "soul," peculiar to itself. My wife and I have had great fun restoring older homes, for our own residence, to what we felt was the nature and character of the building. But, when you own an invest-ment building, you have to do cruel, heartless things to it. Cruel things from painting it all a neutral color, all the way to converting a mansion into apartments, or even tearing a mansion down. You may need to leave a run-down property in a run-down condition. You may need to rent buildings to people to live in that you never in the world would consider living in yourself. You may find yourself financing buildings to the hilt (which you would never do on your own home), and under certain circumstances, you may possibly elect to default and allow foreclosure. These are cruel, horrible things to do to a building which has its own character and its own "soul."

If you walk into a building and its soul starts to speak to you, turn around and walk out. **If you love it, leave it.**

Some of the worst trouble we ever got into involved a house we loved. It was an old classic Victorian mansion with a pillared, wrap-around porch. We loved it so much that we decided to rent it out for a short time and then move into it ourselves. Well, we got into trouble with it, but because we loved it so much, we held onto it far longer than was wise. Only on the day before the foreclosure auction did we finally concede defeat and sell it. **If you love it, leave it.**

Chapter 18

PLAY LANDLORD BY THE BOOK

I remember waking up one day, saying to myself, "Yesterday I couldn't spell landlord, today I are one." I soon discovered, as you also will, that there is more involved in the transition from tenant to landlord, or even from land-owner to landlord than in name only.

KNOW YOUR LEASE

I suggest that you immediately start reading leases. There are standard state approved forms that you can find in any stationery store. These may or may not suit your purposes, so read every lease that you can find. Find a form that you like and then memorize it. Maybe not word for word, but become so familiar with your lease form, that it becomes second nature to you. As a landlord, your dealings rise and fall on the basis of your knowledge of your lease.

You will find that there are standard provisions made for cases when a tenant cannot pay his rent on time. These provisions will vary from State to State, but generally there is a grace period during which the tardy tenant can pay his rent if he pays a late penalty with it. After the prescribed grace period, if the tenant has not paid his rent and late penalties, the process of eviction begins. One thing that I strongly recommend is that the terms of the lease, in case of tenant default, be followed precisely and punctually, with no variations from the written lease.

There always is a tendency, especially with the first-time landlord, to be extra lenient, understanding, and emotionally involved with the tenants. The danger in an emotional involvement with tenants is exactly the same as in purchasing an investment with a friend, as discussed in Chapter 3. Your business decisions become clouded by emotion, and emotional involvement hinders the landlord from making decisions that are crucial to his economic survival.

EVICTION PROCESS

No one likes to feel like Snidely Whiplash, and evictions are not a pleasant thing for anybody, but until the eviction is a legal fact, the landlord has no right to occupy his own property. He cannot reclaim what is rightfully his until those tenants are out. The lease agreement has legally given the control of the property to the tenant for the term of the lease. Eviction is only the process the landlord uses to reclaim possession of his own property.

One needn't feel guilty, even when the eviction process is carried out, because safeguards for the tenants are built into the entire eviction procedure. For instance, the landlord cannot legally change the locks on the building, regardless of provocation. The landlord cannot cut off the utilities, even if the landlord himself is paying for them, even if the tenants are wasting the utilities at his expense.

I once owned an "up and down" duplex, and rented them out "utilities paid" (by me). I had occasion to be at the apartment downstairs and I heard water running in the apartment upstairs. I knocked at the upstairs door and no one answered. Obviously, they had forgotten to turn off the water before leaving. Thinking of all the damage water can do to floors, walls, and ceilings in both apartments, I opened the door with my key and walked in. The tenants **were** there. They just hadn't bothered to answer.

I was right. The hot water **was** running in the kitchen sink. The cold water was also running in the kitchen sink, along with both hot and cold water taps wide open in the bathroom sink and both taps wide open in the bathtub. The TV was on, the radio was on, every light and lamp was on (it was midday), the windows were wide open (it was early Autumn), the thermostat was on maximum, the oven was on full blast with the oven door wide open and all four burners on the stove were on high (they were not cooking). Maybe they were miffed at me.

We had not been on good terms recently since their rent was three weeks late again and still not paid. But that afternoon, I lost my composure. I went to the basement and shut off the electricity and the water and locked the basement doors and windows.

Quiz time: In this case, who was in the wrong?
Answer: I was. I had violated the law by turning off the utilities. The tenants were destroying me financially, but **I** was acting illegally. I didn't much care at that point, but legal papers had not been served and the tenant was "protected" by the law against such acts by the landlord.

Another safeguard for the tenants is the fact that, between each step of the legal process there are waiting periods in which the tenant can redeem himself. There is a five day waiting period between the time a notice is posted on the tenant's door and the time any further action is taken to court. There are other waiting periods; two weeks before you can get a court appointment to plead your case, and another seven days or so before the Sheriff can act once the court has made a decision.

All of this is designed to give the tenant every opportunity to make restitution to the landlord or to move out in a peaceable and orderly manner. Finally, after several hassle free weeks (in my state, it's at least 30 days), the tenant's furniture is put out on the curb for him to move away. This means that even after the tenant has not paid his rent and has gone through a 15 day grace period, there are still 30 days of procedure, during which the tenant can occupy the property rent-free. Your tenant knows this better than you do. If you deal from the heart and not from the head, that 30 to 60 days of rent-free living will extend weeks before you can do anything to reclaim your property.

The entire eviction proceeding is stacked in favor of the tenant. So, if you are going to play landlord, **play it by the book**. The tenants wrote that book.

Chapter 19

THE ABOMINABLE SNOWMAN

I recently met a fine family man, who read a real estate investment book and just as I did, got so excited that he ran out immediately and bought a rental property. This is a man who had enough self-confidence to go all the way. He bought as his first investment, a nineteen unit apartment building. He was going to "make it" in a big way.

HIRING MANAGERS

Because he was employed in his own career, he hired a manager to oversee his apartment building. The manager was to collect rents, make deposits, keep records, maintain the building, deal with the tenants, and screen new tenants. The owner relied on this person's experience and judgment, since he himself had never managed a property before.

It may have been helpful for him to remember that he had never hired a manager before, either. This manager abused his new authority and began to terrorize the tenants until several good ones moved away. The bad tenants stayed. All along the manager reported that everything was "just fine."

One particular tenant had to be evicted because he had severely damaged the apartment he was in. The repairs were time-consuming and expensive, but the owner wasn't too discouraged, because the manager already had a new tenant from California. The new tenant moved in and within a few months, the apartment was in worse shape than before. The "new tenant from California" that the manager had arranged was the very same bad tenant they had evicted. The manager had "snowed" the owner.

As is always the case, the true extent of the owner's losses due to this "snowman" manager was not apparent until some time after he was fired and evicted. The manager had snowed him all along in several important and expensive matters.

Before this investor finally sold the apartment building two years later, he had gone through three managers, and finally struggled through the managing himself.

My recommendation is that your first rental property should be small enough that you can manage it yourself in the time available to you. It should be a single family house or a duplex. It should be located close enough to your residence that you can keep an eye on it and drive by it regularly.

To avoid too many children, your first investment property should be no more than three bedrooms. The utilities should be separately metered and paid directly by the tenants, all accounts being in their names.

Rent should be mailed by the tenants to your bank after an arrangement with the trust department of your bank has been made to receive, record and deposit the payments. If this cannot be done, make sure your tenants get no closer to your address than a post office box, to which all rent payments should be mailed. Tenants should never come to your home to pay their rent and it should be made explicitly clear that you are available by phone only in case of emergency. It is not a bad idea to have a separate phone line for your investment business.

It is said that "good fences make good neighbors" and for reasons discussed in more detail in Chapter 18, a proper detachment from your tenants is crucial in a good landlord-tenant relationship. One investor I met feels so strongly about this "critical distance" that when a tenant calls him irresponsibly, in other words, calls him any time other than in extreme emergency of fire or flood, he sternly warns them never to call again, and evicts them forthwith. They committed a "superfluous call." That may be a little harsh. I might warn once and forgive, but evict them on the second call.

All those cliches—"familiarity breeds contempt" and "absence makes the heart grow fonder," etc., were written about landlords and tenants. **Build a good fence between you and your tenants.**

In the case that you have several units or that your rentals are at a distance of more than 15 minutes from your residence, it is strongly recommended that you hire a management company to handle it, rather than an individual "snow man."

I was once asked by a couple, who were transferred overseas with the military, if I, a realtor and friend, would manage the rental of their home while they were gone. I refused politely, of course (see Chapter 3), and suggested a management company. The cost to them would be a half month's rent and 8% of the monthly rent threafter. We figured a cost over one year of $730. They thought that they would save money, however, so they found their own tenant and moved overseas.

The next time I heard from them, they called from Hawaii asking the same question as a year prior. Would I look into their house? The tenants were more than $1,500 behind in their rent and refused to respond to registered mail demands for payment. The additional cost to them of evicting, cleaning, repairing, advertising and re-leasing over such a distance would be even greater yet. The cost of eviction through the management company would have been exactly seven dollars and would have taken place two months, one ulcer, and $1,500 ago. They had to agree with me that they had been "penny wise and pound foolish."

Management over a distance doesn't work. You can't afford not to have a management company handle your tenants, when you get to the point that several of your properties or your rentals are too far away. A company is much less likely to "snow" you than an individual,

because a company will have less reason to. The company
will know how to handle every instance quickly and inex-
pensively. It will also allow you to be free of your emotional involvements you might otherwise have with your
tenants and it will not make mistakes which need to be
"snowed over."

Chapter 20

TAKE NOTES ON YOURSELF

BUSINESS EXPENSES

From the moment you purchase your first investment property, you are a business person and must conduct yourself as such. Your business expenses can be deducted from the proceeds of your business and from your other incomes, but only under certain conditions. You need to provide evidence that your business expenses were indeed business expenses. In many cases, receipts alone are not sufficient to justify deducting the expense. You need to have some daily record of the costs you pay and how the expenses were incurred.

Mileage expenses for your car, for instance, are costs that you can show with receipts and credit card statements, but to justify those costs as business expenses, you need to show the mileage used every day in conducting your business as opposed to mileage for personal use. Because realtors spend a lot of their time in their car, the I.R.S. is particularly strict with them and require daily totals of miles driven; where they went, with whom and why.

Since looking for and purchasing property, managing and selling it is a business that incurs many small daily expenditures, I recommend that a similar daily record be kept of your expenses. This can best be done with the book that you usually keep with you—your appointment book. The forthcoming Pocket Empire System© was designed specifically to meet the daily needs of the real estate investor in acquiring, maintaining, and managing his properties.

You need to take notes on yourself in some organized fashion, but your notes on yourself should not stop with a daily expense record. How often have you been working on an item that you've not been able to conclude in one sitting, and you've had to come back to it after a period of time? Isn't the first thing you say to yourself or to others, "Let's see now, where did we leave this?" Putting everything into writing is one method of avoiding some confusion on this point as we've discussed in another chapter. Taking notes on yourself involves far more than just that. Everyday, important things are said to you over the phone or in person, things whose importance may not become apparent until days, weeks or even months later, at which time you may need to ask yourself, "Now, where did we leave this?" Knowing exactly where, when and with whom you left the matter could be the turning point in a transaction, or even in a legal case for you.

In your business dealings you need to keep an accurate

record of communications. The content of telephone calls is particularly subject to modification in your memory, because of the visual and other-sensory distractions which are competing for your attention during the call. You need to write into a daily record for permanent keeping who you spoke with, by name, when you spoke with them and what information was conveyed to and from you.

Any information conveyed verbally still may be hearsay evidence in a legal sense, but if you can show a record keeping system in which each discussion is a matter of written record, your testimony will be much more believable to the court or the I.R.S. In rather traumatic dealings with a second trust lender, which I will relate in following chapters when most appropriate, the importance of memory-enhancing daily notes was borne out to me.

I had called the lender two months earlier, discussing with him a pay-off figure and our initial disagreement arose from that phone conversation. A month later, in that same case, I called an attorney and asked him to do certain things. He called me back and told me the results of those inquiries which I had asked him to make. I, of course, didn't make any record of those telephone conversations or the content of those phone calls. (I hadn't read this chapter yet.) When the matter became very much legal, I found myself in the awkward position of having to say, "Remember two months ago, when I spoke with you on the phone, you told me such and such?" Part of the case became my word against his word, which is of no value in a court of law.

The lender had a good habit of jotting down on little sheets of paper, all telephone conversations he had with people he had loaned money to. He looked in the file folder with my name on it and discovered that he had failed to take notes on that telephone call received from me two months earlier. At that point I was kicking myself because I had no written record to refute his notion that I had not called him at all. My record could have spoken against his record to some effect. Of course, the case did not hang on these evidences, the value of which being negligible anyway, but at least I would have seemed much more credible. I could have looked up that date, and said, "On this date, at this time, I called you and we discussed thus and so, and you said such." All of that, I could have said on the strength of notes I had taken, rather than merely on the strength of my memory of those occasions.

TAKE A PERSON'S NAME

One day I was observing a friend of mine, who is in politics on Capitol Hill, as he was making an inquiry of an office worker somewhere. He was particularly careful to get the name of that person, the full name, that is, including the correct spelling. As he was talking, he took notes on what that person said. Taking that person's name accomplished several things. First of all, if he needed to make subsequent calls, he could ask for that person and begin the conversation where they left off the first time. If he had ended up having to talk with someone else, he would have had to start his story over again from the beginning.

Furthermore, when a person is asked his name, he will

be more careful to give accurate information because he knows he is responsible for that information and is no longer anonymous. I remember someone suggesting to me that many of the problems of modern industry could be resolved if each factory worker were required to sign every piece of work that he processed. Each worker would be much more careful to do a good job when processing his own work. Information is a product, and offices are factories. **Make people "sign" their names to the information they give you.**

One more, and possibly the most important aspect of taking someone's name is that you can use that name. Sales people are taught the importance of knowing and using a person's name. No word in the language is more beautiful and welcome to a person than the proper use of his own name. If you use a person's name often when you talk to him you'll not only keep his attention (remember the distractions during a telephone call) but you will also keep his affections. So using a person's name correctly and frequently will help you get what you want.

When you talk with someone on the phone, take notes on yourself—ask their name, and use it often. When I talk with successful managers, I'm interested in finding that they habitually use this principle. "Yes, Mr. Sandberg. Did you know, Mr. Sandberg, that...." And when they are through, it's always, "Thank you for calling Mr. Sandberg." I know that they would never remember my name except that they have written it down, but that courtesy feels very good to me.

The great value in having all of this information written

down as you get it on a day by day basis (and written down in one central location, for instance, the The Pocket Empire©), is that months later, when you need to begin communicating again with a person or an agency, you can go back quickly and accurately to the day you initiated the communication and recall people's names while reviewing the information that was conveyed. Then, with accuracy and full faculty of knowledge, you can communicate again on a friendly and cordial basis. Take notes on yourself and keep those notes in a system of some sort, which allows you immediate access. You will never again have to say, "Well, let's see, where did we leave this?"

Being able to recite precisely and accurately where all negotiations were left will give you the upper hand in your dealings. You won't forget what was agreed to and you won't allow the other person to forget.

Chapter 21

AVOID LAWYERS
LIKE DEATH

The very moment you begin dealing in contracts, or dealing with money, you will begin to have disagreements about the amounts of money due and when they are due, or what act or omission is required by the contract. Someone will argue that he doesn't owe you the money that you think he owes, or that you owe him more money than you feel you do. Depending on your tolerance and communication skills, you may be able to discuss your differences intelligently.

SETTLING DISPUTES

The trouble is that many disputes about money or other contractual agreements last longer than our tolerance level or our ability to communicate. When we can no longer communicate intelligently, the first unintellegent thing we usually do is go get a lawyer.

The reason it is so unintelligent is that from the very moment you even breath the word "lawyer" into your disagreement with someone else, communication stops. Anger and hurt feelings intensify because the element of legal force has now been introduced. Granted, through the sheer weight of law, you may be able to force compliance, but you can never force agreement. Any kind of a forced compliance will be carried out grudgingly and spitefully and further financial or physical damage may be wrought by the party who is forced into compliance.

I had to evict a tenant once, after weeks and weeks of real financial and physical damage had been inflicted upon my property. Because the situation was so emotionally charged on both sides, the tenant although gone before the full eviction process had been served, left the house in very poor condition. He stole certain items of mine which were on the property as well.

When I mentioned it to a county health inspector, who was at the house subsequent to that, he told me, "You're lucky. You got off easy." I answered sarcastically, "Sure, I got off easy, I should be grateful." He said, "Yes," and related to me a couple of experiences he had had in his brief career with the county, in which the tenants, who were evicted, left the property, but left a fire in it, which inflicted severe fire damage to the building. These fires were officially fires of suspicious origin, and couldn't be proven to be started by the ousted tenants. The county inspector explained to me, however, that coincidences of this sort happen far too frequently.

Maybe I was lucky that my tenant didn't burn the place down. Evicted tenants are wounded animals and are best dealt with in a cool and detached manner, strictly according to the letter of the law and under the auspices of the local sheriff. As I think back on this situation, I remember having been offered a compromise of some sort just prior to my "calling in the law." This compromise was unacceptable at the time. When I rejected the compromise offer, it was withdrawn, communication stopped, and the situation grew markedly worse.

The same thing happens when you get an attorney. At that very moment, communication stops. The first response of the other party is, "Well, if you're getting an attorney, then I'll get an attorney." At that point, the disagreement is out of the hands of the parties involved, and under the control of the attorneys.

BRINGING IN AN ATTORNEY

A funny thing happens to numbers when an attorney joins in the dispute. You've got to figure that any time you have a sum of money you've disagreed upon, that amount will at least double the moment you turn it over to an attorney. At that point, the money that is outstanding will be the original amount plus attorney's fees on your side, plus attorney's fees on the other side.

Now all of a sudden, there are four parties in the dispute, who each have a vested monetary interest in the outcome of the disagreement. Without fail that additional monetary interest will put the sum of money beyond the reach of the parties involved. In other words, a compromise reconciliation between the disagreeing parties is not only unlikely, but may be even impossible.

The way attorneys in some cases figure their interest in the monetary outcome of the case is very interesting. They don't always charge fees for services rendered based on the services actually rendered. Sometimes they will charge fees based on a percentage of the amounts collected.

A lender with whom we had a substantial disagreement on amounts due, refused to listen to our complaints and took the hardline position that we really did owe him more than we thought we had agreed to. My talking to him and pointing out the simple mistake and the simple remedy produced no change in his position. I, therefore, went to the attorney who had originally prepared the papers some time before. I asked him to point out the error to the lender. The lender's answer was exactly the same.

I went to another attorney just to see if an uninvolved third party could force the lender to listen to reason. As that lawyer looked at the papers and heard my story, he said, "This is usury. If he maintains that you owe him that much, then according to the terms of the note, he has charged an interest rate in excess of that allowed by the law. We've got him on usury."

This attorney explained further that the penalties for usury prescribed by the law, which may not be declined, nor moderated in any way by the victim of the usury, were that the entire loan amount would be forgiven and all of the interest paid by the victim of usury would be doubled and paid back by the usurious lender. That came to a total penalty of $27,500.

My intention in going to that attorney to begin with was to shelter myself from being overcharged by the amount of $750. Now all of a sudden, the sum of money involved was $27,500! I told the attorney, "I don't want to stick it to this guy; all I want him to do is be reasonable."

The attorney said, "O.K. We'll see how reasonable he is when he's served with papers."

In a few days, a very formal and legally composed letter was sent demanding $27,500. Immediately, as you can imagine, there was a response from the lender, the lender's attorney and from friends of the lender. One evening, even the lender called me and we talked face-to-face (face-to-ear?) for some time. I was chuckling to myself all the while, thinking, "Finally, he's being reasonable, isn't it wonderful?"

I called my lawyer and told him, that the lender wanted to make reconciliation. He said, "Of course you told him that it's out of your hands." I said I had told him that I had to consult with my attorney first. My lawyer said, " That was exactly the right thing to do." As we discussed a possible settlement out of court, I suggested that the lender pay the legal costs incurred. He said, "Yes, I have a vested interest in the case. You can tell him that."

Later in that same conversation, my attorney said, "My share of the collected penalties will be $3,500. If he's going to settle, he's going to have to satisfy my interest."

My jaw just about dropped off of my face. The "compromise" settlement figure now became $4,250. In addition, the attorney suggested that because of the hassle I had gone through, I ought to be offered some further monetary consideration from the lender.

The outcome was that although the lender agreed to compromise a sum of $750, he was totally unprepared to compromise the sum of $5,000. He got his lawyer involved and we went to court. I was put in the silly position of having to sue for something I really didn't want just to satisfy the interests of persons who were not parties to the original dispute to begin with.

This sort of experience has lead me and other investors I know to put it this way: Attorneys create more problems than they solve; or, your problems only just start when attorneys get involved.

There are, however, beneficial ways to use the knowledge of the real estate attorneys and their access to the legal system. As I mentioned in other chapters, it is important to check with real estate attorneys about specific details of the code in your particular state, the legality of questionable transactions, and other points of loss. Generally speaking, it's not hard to find an attorney who is not reticent to discuss a particular point of law with you over the telephone without charge to you.

REVIEW CONTRACT WITH ATTORNEY

As a realtor, from time to time, I would run across

buyers, who were hesitant to submit a contract for purchase without having "their attorney look at it" first. Of course, I recognize that response as simply indicating a reluctance or inability on their part to make a decision for themselves. They were looking for someone else to make the decision for them at the time they asked their lawyer to review their purchase proposal contract.

Should you, as a buyer or seller, ever feel the need to have an attorney review a contract, it is important to remember this: If an attorney looks at the terms of the contract and says, "This is a good deal, go with it," and the project becomes a bit loser, the attorney has become a party to the contract by advising his client to go ahead with it. His client, since he based his decision in the transaction on the advice of the attorney, could sue the attorney. No attorney in the world will knowingly put himself in a position of liability by recommending an action based on a contract which was submitted to him for review.

All an attorney can and will do is review the legal form of the contract and render an opinion on the legal form and not on the content of the contract. Often, an attorney will feel the need to justify the fee he will be charging to review the form. As a result, he will make some minor change in the language of the contract. Since any unilateral change in the face of a contract makes that contract voidable by the other party, this sort of meddling in the language of the contract can put the whole transaction in jeopardy.

A lot of money is spent on the preparation of blank documents by real estate companies, who publish them. Their own attorneys review them for legal content and for compliance with appropriate state requirements before the blank form is ever approved for publication. Each company has a different contract form, so it is still reasonable to assume that if you gave a particular form to five lawyers to review, you'd get five different responses to the form.

The point to remember is that if an attorney responds at all in reviewing a contract or proposal, the response will be necessarily non-committal, because he cannot afford the liability of becoming a party to the transaction. Furthermore, if he does make some change, it will be a change in legal language which has nothing to do with the terms of the contract.

So, avoid attorneys like death. If the person with whom you have a dispute will not conform to your arguments through a concern for fairness and honesty, then you compromise. In that case you're not the loser." You are in reality avoiding a much greater loss than you are conceding. If he will not respond favorably to compromise, then concede entirely to his point of view. If the loss in conceding is too great, then in a tactful and non-threatening way, suggest that you would really rather not call attorneys in on the matter. (In other words, threaten him.) Don everything you possibly can and some things you can't do, **but avoid attorneys like death.**

Chapter 22

DEATH COMES TO US ALL

It may happen that you will have a disagreement with someone who will not compromise and the amounts involved are too great to simply concede. If a casual mention that you don't want to have to get an attorney involved does not bring you to terms, and you're forced to get legal help, get an attorney.

HIRE A GOOD ATTORNEY

Get the most flambouyant, highest priced, "Broadway Joe" type of attorney you can find. This may seem like strange advice coming from someone who doesn't have money to burn, but I tried it the other way. Once, when we were faced with an action that we thought we could legally avoid or forestall, I went shopping for an attorney. The way I shopped was to ask them how much they charged. I found one who I thought was quite reasonable in his hourly charge for consultation. So, I went to him.

His waiting room was small, dark and smelled bad. It had been paneled poorly in dark, cheap paneling. It had a smoke-stained acoustical tile ceiling with recessed lighting through plastic panes. Next to the old black vinyl couch, was a standing lamp, decorated with dusty, artificial flowers.

The attorney had greasy hair, nicotine stained teeth, dirt under his fingernails, and when he reached across the table, he revealed a ripped seam in his jacket, and that jacket, incidentally, clashed with his trousers.

As I explained my situation, several times during the course of my morning, he excused himself from the room and left me alone. During one of those absences from the room, I perused his book case, and pulled out a volume of the state statutes I thought to be appropriate to my case. Thumbing through it, I found a section of the code that spoke directly to our problem. As he came back into the room I put the volume back. After a few more minutes of talking, he went over to the bookshelf, pulled out the same volume, thumbed to the same page, and started reading. My thoughts at that point were, "My goodness, he ought to be more familiar with the code than I am." In all fairness, he probably was, but it was a little disheartening that he would have to look up the code before he could answer my questions and make suggestions.

I was in his office about four hours that morning, and

felt very frustrated as I left. A few days later, on a friend's recommendation, I went to a legal office of a different sort. It was in a modern high-rise building in the heart of Washington, D.C. There were four partners' names in brass letters on the massive oak doors that opened into their lobby. I sat in a leather sofa, my feet on oriental carpets, looking at the solid cherry paneling. I thought to myself, "I wonder how much this carpet is going to cost me. I can't afford to be here."

Later, reflecting back, I realized how I couldn't afford not to be there. A young, energetic, bright lawyer met me in the lobby, and walked back into his office with me. He was not one of the four names on the door, but immediately I was aware that he knew his business, which was real estate law. As I explained my situation, he asked a few questions and told me exactly where I stood, according to the codes. He offered a suggestion or two, and called in another equally energetic young, bright attorney to see if there were any other angles from which to attack the problem. He told me exactly the methods he would pursue, what he hoped to accomplish, and furthermore, just plain leveled with me. He told me that because my legal position was almost non-existent and they might not be able to defend me on legal grounds, they would at least jump up on the table and do a song and dance, to buy me the time I needed to work myself out of the situation I was in. I left the office within two hours of when I entered. The total bill was less than the four hours of fumbling around I did with the cut-rate attorney I had first consulted. I spent less money, getting more done, with a much greater prospect of success. As I've reflected since that time on this phenomenon, it really only stands to reason that the brightest attorneys will be working for the firms which offer enough money to attract the best people to work for them.

If you must retain an attorney, don't try to save money on legal costs. Hire "Broadway Joe."

Chapter 23

NEUTRALIZE

In some states a settlement attorney is used to settle a real estate transaction. His responsibilities are to prepare and process the paperwork required by the lender and by the state. He also sees that all terms of the contract are met and dispurses the funds. His job, simply put, is to represent the contract.

SELLING AGENT

In a normal residential transaction, there is a "listing agent" who helps the seller of the house, a "selling agent" who helps the buyer of the house, and the attorney remains neutral. In case of any conflict or disagreement, the attorney serves only to formalize whatever adjustments need to be made to the original transaction. He cannot defend the interests of one party or the other in any case.

What I've described is ideal. In other words, that's the way it should be. But, it isn't always the case. If you are a purchaser, working with a real estate agent to help you make the purchase, you need to realize that that agent, as helpful as he has been in making your purchase, is being paid by the seller.

The seller agrees with the listing broker to pay a certain commission as compensation for the service of marketing and selling the house under certain terms. When the listing agent enters that house into the multiple listing system, and places a "For Sale" sign in front of the house, he is inviting all other licensed real estate agents in the state to help him sell that house for the seller. When an eventual sale is consummated, the commission is split between the listing agency (working primarily with the seller) and the selling agency (working primarily with the buyer). Despite all outward appearances, the selling agent, who works with the buyer, is legally obligated to uphold the interest of the seller in all cases.

AGENT DOES NOT REPRESENT BUYER

If the selling agent can persuade the prospective purchaser to make an offer that is more advantageous to the seller, he is legally obligated to do that. You, the buyer, then, cannot expect to have your real estate agent look out for your best interest in case of dispute. All the agents are on the seller's side. It is a very lonely feeling to have trouble surface at the settlement table when you realize that the agents are all representing the seller, and the attorney is neutral. Indeed, the attorney may have been hired by the seller to do the settlement and must represent the seller in that case. No one is representing you.

Only when retained as a "buyer's broker" and paid directly by the buyer, as discussed in Chapter 4, does an agent represent the buyer's interest at all.

For that reason, perhaps it is generally the right of the buyer to select the settlement attorney. You, as buyer must exercise that right in order to insure that the lawyer is indeed neutral. Many times, even in the listing agreement with his broker, the seller will express his choice of attorneys. You should avoid this situation. Suggest that, since you are also paying part of the attorney's fees, an attorney of your choice should do the settlement. If the seller is insistent, suggest that the seller retain his attorney at his expense, of course, to sit in on the settlement but **not** handle the case. You **must** neutralize.

POWER PLAY

We namely avoided what might have been a disaster by taking the precaution to neutralize what was becoming a "power play" by the other parties involved in a deal. We saw it coming and took action to prevent trouble. We were an interested third party in a transaction between a buyer and a seller. In other words, we had equity above the seller's pay-off figure that would be paid at the settlement, so we had to be there. But for some time prior to the appointed settlement, there was a dispute as to exactly what that seller's pay-off figure would be. It would have to be resolved once and for all at the settlement table.

In our state, the buyer has the right to select the attorney to handle the case. The buyer was a partnership, working through a trustee. The trustee happened to be a real estate attorney, so they asked their own trustee to be the settlement attorney in the case. Fortunately, we happened to discover that the seller's personal attorney was one and the same person as the buyer's trustee and settlement attorney. We couldn't believe it. In a case where it was predetermined that there would be a dispute about pay-off figures, we would be the only ones not represented by legal counsel—the only ones not represented by the same attorney, who controlled the disbursement of funds. We saw trouble coming.

We called in an attorney, a high priced lawyer at that, just to sit in on the meeting, to protect our interest by being sure that nothing irregular happened. He didn't actually add anything to the proceedings or change any numbers on the settlement sheet, but there is no doubt in my mind that his being there was a controlling influence on the proceedings. Proper disbursements were made.

Of course, bringing in your own attorney on every transaction could become very expensive very fast. Having our own legal man at that settlement cost us about $300, but it probably saved us about ten times that amount in money that was at risk.

Any time a settlement attorney is selected, be sure that that settlement attorney is neutral and can represent the contract without allegiance to the other party. You might find it advantageous to keep an attorney on call, so if there is a dispute at the settlement table, a quick call to your lawyer could save a lot of time and money. If your attorney is not available when the dispute arises, take a hike. Don't forget what we discussed in Chapter 16. It is not unusual to adjourn briefly while outside counsel is sought.

Chapter 24

DON'T DO IT TOO WELL

It used to be said that, because real estate is such a tremendous investment, for every dollar that you put into improving a property, you'll get two or three dollars out when it's time to sell. I don't believe, without reservation, that that is so.

STAY IN PRICE FRAME

In any particular neighborhood, there is a price frame dictated by traditional demand for that neighborhood. A bell curve can also be shown to reflect selling prices in that neighborhood. The greatest number of sales in any area will be right in the middle price range, between the high priced and the low-priced houses. Fewer buyers want the cheapest house in a neighborhood because it may be small or run down. There are also fewer buyers looking for the most expensive house in the neighborhood. Generally those buyers go on to the more expensive areas of town and buy a middle priced house in the more expensive neighborhood. Most buyers are looking for the mid-range houses.

One great tendency among investors who want to buy, fix up and sell again, is to overimprove thinking that the higher the price, the more money they'll make. They improve a home so dramatically that its price is pushed beyond the bell curve of buyers. The house, then, becomes harder to sell.

The last thing you want to have happen to you is to be stuck holding a number of properties that will not sell. One way to insure that they will not sell is to overimprove for the neighborhood. Builders sometimes fall prey to this kind of thinking. They may say, "But what I build and sell reflects so much about me, I want it to be first class." But Baloney. What you sell reflects the market to which you are selling. How quickly it sells is an indication of how close you have come to the market that you have targeted. Consider carefully the market that you are selling to. It has been said that the only things that appeal to tenants, and for that matter, the only things that appeal to buyers of personal residences, are paint and carpeting. Whereas, all that appeals to the investor-buyer is the profit-and-loss paperwork.

If you are selling a multi-unit building, that is, one with two or more apartments in it, don't concern yourself with cosmetics. Presenting a property that needs cosmetic work would actually be to the seller's advantage, since the buyer will need to make cosmetic improvements in order to justify raising rents. Furthermore, if the buyer does not have the cash necessary for the cosmetic improvements, he will say so in his purchase proposal to you. You may want to use those potential cosmetic improvements as a bargaining tool in your favor.

The best way to prepare that property for sale to an investor is to prepare the paperwork. Put all the overhead costs, the utility costs, costs of carrying as well as all information on the existing financing, warranties, maintenance contracts, management contracts, leases, balance sheets, profit and loss statements, etc., into one package that is clear and concise.

I suggest also that sellers of any rental property, especially multi-unit types, do not renew leases as they expire. Rent only on a month-to-month basis when preparing to sell your building. The new owner will only be able to justify paying the price you ask, if he can change the rents accordingly and he cannot change the rents of unexpired leases. If the property is a single family residence that you have had rented, repaint the interior of the house, put in new carpeting, clean the kitchen, the bathrooms, and all of the glass, and sell it to a residential buyer. Remember, when you're contemplating making improvements, make the fewest improvements you can to bring it up to the middle of the market, no higher.

HIGHEST PRICE POSSIBLE

One other consideration when you're selling; the temptation is to list it for the highest price possible, because it is "worth it," and because you want to hold out for top dollar. I've included here, for your consideration, a table showing the relative values of a dollar now and the value of that same dollar in the future. It is a fact that, even when not counting inflation, but only considering the use to which you could put that money in the meantime (assuming a possible 12% rate of return), each dollar that you could get today is worth only $.78 if you have to wait two years to get it. That same dollar received today and invested at 12% would be worth $1.25. Either way you figure it, you have to get 25% more money two years later to receive the same value.

Remember again, that your money is made when you buy—not when you sell. So the few extra dollars that you may be holding out for now can actually get in the way of another profitable purchase. Truly, a bird in the hand now is worth $1.25 in the bush. Take a little less than the "market value," but by all means, take it now.

The house that we were living in in Virginia was in a 55 year old neighborhood. The house was a large colonial, in a neighborhood of large colonials, and when we bought it, it had a lot of room for improvement. The owner from whom we purchased it had converted the house from two apartments back into one residence, as it had originally been built. When we bought it, we took it from there and of course, reflecting our own taste, we put in every improvement feasible; a new heating system, central air conditioning, a new kitchen, new bathrooms, new plumbing and wiring throughout. We converted a screened porch into a sunroom/family room, and built a deck on the back. When we decided to move and it came time to sell, we discovered that we had pushed the value of that house up to the top 10% of the neighborhood. We were repeatedly assured by real estate agents, principal brokers, and my own research, that the house was worth between $125,000 and $132,000. I'm sure it was worth it. There were houses four blocks away in a slightly more prestigeous area, with less room and less improvements that were on the market for $139,000.

We had a great deal of trouble marketing our home, as desirable as it was, because the neighborhood did not support the price of the house. It wasn't that much more expensive than anything that had sold in the neighborhood before then, but it was just enough higher to delay the sale of the home. Nothing else had sold for more than $120,000 in the last year. We waited and waited and finally sold it for $119,000.

There was some value to holding it, because we were still living in it, but had it been an investment property, we would have had to drop the price more dramatically in order to sell it within a reasonable amount of time. Don't get caught overimproving for the neighborhood. Stay away from the top 10% and the bottom 10% in any given neighborhood. **Sell your house where the buyers are, and that's the middle price range for your neighborhood.**

PRESENT VALUE OF $1.00
RETURNED IN THE FUTURE

YEAR	6%	7%	8%	9%	10%	11%	12%	13%	14%	15%	16%	17%	18%	19%	20%
1	0.94	0.93	0.92	0.91	0.90	0.89	0.89	0.88	0.88	0.87	0.86	0.85	0.85	0.84	0.83
2	0.89	0.87	0.86	0.84	0.83	0.81	0.78	0.78	0.77	0.76	0.74	0.73	0.72	0.71	0.69
3	0.84	0.82	0.79	0.77	0.75	0.73	0.71	0.69	0.67	0.66	0.64	0.62	0.61	0.59	0.58
4	0.79	0.76	0.74	0.71	0.68	0.66	0.64	0.61	0.59	0.57	0.55	0.53	0.52	0.50	0.48
5	0.75	0.71	0.68	0.65	0.62	0.59	0.57	0.54	0.52	0.50	0.47	0.46	0.44	0.42	0.40
6	0.70	0.67	0.63	0.60	0.56	0.53	0.51	0.48	0.46	0.43	0.41	0.39	0.37	0.35	0.33
7	0.67	0.62	0.58	0.55	0.51	0.48	0.45	0.43	0.40	0.38	0.36	0.33	0.31	0.30	0.28
8	0.63	0.58	0.54	0.50	0.47	0.43	0.40	0.38	0.35	0.33	0.31	0.28	0.27	0.25	0.23
9	0.59	0.54	0.50	0.46	0.42	0.39	0.36	0.33	0.31	0.29	0.26	0.24	0.23	0.21	0.19
10	0.56	0.51	0.46	0.42	0.39	0.35	0.32	0.29	0.27	0.25	0.23	0.21	0.20	0.18	0.16
11	0.53	0.48	0.43	0.39	0.35	0.32	0.29	0.26	0.24	0.21	0.20	0.18	0.16	0.15	0.13
12	0.50	0.44	0.40	0.36	0.32	0.29	0.26	0.23	0.21	0.19	0.17	0.15	0.14	0.12	0.11
13	0.47	0.41	0.37	0.33	0.29	0.26	0.23	0.20	0.18	0.16	0.15	0.13	0.12	0.10	0.09
14	0.44	0.39	0.34	0.30	0.26	0.23	0.20	0.18	0.16	0.14	0.13	0.11	0.10	0.09	0.08
15	0.42	0.36	0.32	0.27	0.24	0.21	0.18	0.16	0.14	0.13	0.11	0.09	0.08	0.07	0.06
16	0.39	0.34	0.29	0.25	0.22	0.19	0.16	0.14	0.13	0.11	0.09	0.08	0.07	0.06	0.05
17	0.37	0.32	0.27	0.23	0.20	0.17	0.15	0.13	0.11	0.09	0.08	0.07	0.06	0.05	0.05
18	0.35	0.30	0.25	0.21	0.18	0.15	0.13	0.11	0.10	0.08	0.07	0.06	0.05	0.04	0.04
19	0.33	0.28	0.23	0.19	0.16	0.14	0.12	0.10	0.08	0.07	0.06	0.05	0.04	0.04	0.03
20	0.31	0.26	0.21	0.18	0.15	0.12	0.10	0.09	0.07	0.06	0.05	0.04	0.04	0.03	0.03
21	0.29	0.24	0.20	0.16	0.14	0.11	0.09	0.08	0.06	0.05	0.04	0.04	0.03	0.03	0.02
22	0.28	0.23	0.18	0.15	0.13	0.10	0.08	0.07	0.06	0.05	0.04	0.03	0.03	0.02	0.02
23	0.26	0.21	0.17	0.14	0.11	0.09	0.07	0.06	0.05	0.04	0.03	0.03	0.02	0.02	0.02
24	0.25	0.20	0.16	0.13	0.10	0.08	0.07	0.05	0.04	0.03	0.02	0.02	0.02	0.02	0.01
25	0.23	0.18	0.15	0.12	0.09	0.07	0.06	0.05	0.04	0.03	0.02	0.02	0.02	0.01	0.01
26	0.22	0.17	0.14	0.11	0.08	0.06	0.05	0.04	0.03	0.03	0.02	0.02	0.01	0.01	0.01
27	0.21	0.16	0.13	0.10	0.08	0.06	0.05	0.04	0.03	0.02	0.02	0.01	0.01	0.01	0.01
28	0.20	0.15	0.12	0.09	0.07	0.05	0.04	0.03	0.03	0.02	0.01	0.01	0.01	0.01	0.01
29	0.18	0.14	0.11	0.08	0.06	0.05	0.04	0.03	0.02	0.02	0.01	0.01	0.01	0.01	0.01
30	0.17	0.13	0.10	0.07	0.06	0.04	0.03	0.02	0.02	0.02	0.01	0.01	0.01	0.01	0.01

EXAMPLE: You are going to receive a lump sum payment of $15,000 ten years in the future. If you could invest that money now at 12%, how much will that $15,000 be worth when received ten years from now?

Find the present value factor for ten years at 12% = 0.32. Multiply that factor by the future amount $15,000 = $4,800. The present value of $15,000 due 10 years from now is only $4,800.

FUTURE VALUE TABLE
$1 AT COMPOUND INTEREST

YEAR	6%	7%	8%	9%	10%	11%	12%	13%	14%	15%	16%	17%	18%	19%	20%
1	1.06	1.07	1.08	1.09	1.10	1.11	1.12	1.13	1.14	1.15	1.16	1.17	1.18	1.19	1.20
2	1.12	1.14	1.17	1.19	1.21	1.23	1.25	1.28	1.30	1.32	1.35	1.37	1.39	1.42	1.44
3	1.19	1.23	1.26	1.30	1.33	1.37	1.40	1.44	1.48	1.52	1.56	1.60	1.64	1.69	1.73
4	1.26	1.31	1.36	1.41	1.46	1.52	1.57	1.63	1.69	1.75	1.81	1.87	1.94	2.01	2.07
5	1.34	1.40	1.47	1.54	1.61	1.68	1.76	1.84	1.93	2.01	2.10	2.19	2.29	2.39	2.49
6	1.42	1.50	1.59	1.68	1.77	1.87	1.97	2.08	2.20	2.31	2.44	2.57	2.70	2.84	2.99
7	1.50	1.61	1.71	1.83	1.95	2.08	2.21	2.35	2.50	2.66	2.83	3.00	3.19	3.38	3.58
8	1.59	1.72	1.85	1.99	2.14	2.30	2.48	2.66	2.85	3.06	3.28	3.51	3.76	4.02	4.30
9	1.69	1.84	2.00	2.17	2.36	2.56	2.77	3.00	3.25	3.52	3.80	4.11	4.44	4.79	5.16
10	1.79	1.90	2.16	2.37	2.60	2.84	3.11	3.39	3.71	4.05	4.41	4.81	5.23	5.69	6.19
11	1.90	2.10	2.33	2.58	2.85	3.15	3.48	3.84	4.23	4.65	5.12	5.62	6.18	6.78	7.43
12	2.01	2.25	2.52	2.81	3.14	3.50	3.90	4.33	4.82	5.35	5.94	6.58	7.29	8.06	8.92
13	2.13	2.41	2.72	3.07	3.45	3.88	4.36	4.90	5.49	6.15	6.89	7.70	8.60	9.60	10.70
14	2.26	2.58	2.94	3.34	3.80	4.31	4.89	5.53	6.26	7.08	7.99	9.01	10.15	11.42	12.84
15	2.40	2.76	3.17	3.64	4.18	4.78	5.47	6.25	7.14	8.14	9.27	10.54	11.97	13.59	15.41
16	2.54	2.95	3.43	3.97	4.60	5.31	6.13	7.07	8.14	9.36	10.75	12.33	14.13	16.17	18.49
17	2.69	3.16	3.70	4.33	5.05	5.90	6.87	7.99	9.28	10.76	12.47	14.43	16.67	19.24	22.19
18	2.85	3.38	4.00	4.72	5.56	6.54	7.69	9.02	10.58	12.38	14.46	16.88	19.67	22.90	26.62
19	3.03	3.62	4.32	5.14	6.12	7.26	8.61	10.20	12.06	14.23	16.78	19.75	23.21	27.25	31.95
20	3.21	3.87	4.66	5.60	6.73	8.06	9.65	11.52	13.74	16.37	19.46	23.11	27.39	32.43	38.34
21	3.40	4.14	5.03	6.11	7.40	8.95	10.80	13.02	15.67	18.82	22.57	27.03	32.32	38.59	46.00
22	3.60	4.43	5.43	6.66	8.14	9.93	12.10	14.71	17.86	21.64	26.19	31.63	38.14	45.92	55.21
23	3.82	4.74	5.87	7.26	8.95	11.02	13.55	16.63	20.36	24.89	30.38	37.01	45.01	54.65	66.25
24	4.04	5.07	6.34	7.91	9.85	12.24	15.18	18.79	23.21	28.62	35.24	43.30	53.11	65.03	79.50
25	4.29	5.43	6.85	8.62	10.83	13.59	17.00	21.23	26.46	32.92	40.87	50.66	62.67	77.39	95.40
26	4.54	5.81	7.40	9.40	11.92	15.08	19.04	23.99	30.17	37.86	47.41	59.27	73.95	92.09	114.47
27	4.82	6.21	7.99	10.24	13.11	16.74	21.32	27.11	34.39	43.53	55.00	69.38	87.26	109.50	137.38
28	5.11	6.65	8.63	11.17	14.42	18.58	23.88	30.63	39.20	50.07	63.80	81.13	102.96	130.41	164.84
29	5.42	7.11	9.32	12.17	15.86	20.62	26.75	34.62	44.69	57.57	74.00	94.92	121.50	155.19	197.81
30	5.74	7.61	10.06	13.27	17.45	22.89	29.96	39.11	50.95	66.21	85.85	111.06	143.37	184.67	237.27

EXAMPLE: How much will a $15,000 investment be worth in 10 years at 12% interest compounded? Locate the future value factor above for 12% interest, at 10 years: 3.11 and multiply it by $15,000. 3.11 X $15,000 = $46,650.00.

Chapter 25

THE PAPER GAME

There are all sorts of terms under which you can sell your property. You could sell it for all cash. As we discussed in the last chapter, the advantage to this option is that cash now is worth less a year from now. However, it is unlikely in today's market, that your buyer will bring in all cash, or refinance the entire amount without asking you to hold back paper.

CASH FOR EQUITY

Taking all cash for the equity in your house might be disadvantageous to you anyway. A big bundle of cash taken all at once, may be rather difficult to handle for tax purposes. Of course, if your cash taken out of a sale is a long-term capital gain, only 40% is taxable income anyway, but that additional 40%, added to whatever other income you might have, may very well bump you up over your existing tax bracket. The consequences are apparent and holding a note for some of your equity is one way to avoid this.

Ask yourself this question: "Would you rather have a million dollars, or would you rather have what a million dollars can do for you?" I think there's really no question of the advantages of having a million dollars working for you at a reasonable rate of return. That's the whole philosophy behind building a real estate empire. For only the **cash down payment and the cost of holding the property,** the investor can literally have a million dollars of value working for him, appreciating and drawing income. He doesn't have and never did have the million dollars, but he controls the earning power of a million dollars.

HOLD PAPER

I'd venture to say that if I gave you a million dollars, the first thing you'd do with it is immediately invest it in something that will pay you a monthly income. When you sell a house, and take back part of your equity in a note, paying a certain rate of interest, what you have actually done is taken from the buyer all of that equity in cash, and loaned it back to him at that rate of interest. Of course, your loan back to the purchaser is secured by the property, and your interest in the property is recorded in the land records of the county. It may be to your advantage, then, to hold paper rather than to take cash...if you do it wisely.

I once heard of a real estate agent, who, in order to complete the sale of a house, talked the sellers into taking back their equity in a ten year note. That's fine, except that the sellers were seventy-five years old. What made it worse, was the fact that the ten year note was assumable, so there was literally no chance of ever collecting on the note before the due date. Those people had no business taking back paper. I could have shot the agent who convinced them to do that. You may also have no business taking back paper, depending on your situation, so think it through carefully. If you take back paper, look carefully at the terms to be sure that they fit your needs.

I suggest as a general rule that you do hold financing, but only under certain terms. First of all, if you can avoid it, make the note non-assumable. Talk to a real estate attorney over the telephone, and ask him if in your state, as in the State of Virginia, any note is assumable unless there is language to the contrary in the face of the note. In other words, any note is assumable, unless it states otherwise. If that is the case in your state, be sure to add language to the note to make it non-assumable. Get the buyer to agree to this stipulation before you accept a proposal for purchase. If the buyer has in his mind that the note you'll be taking back is assumable, and you have in your mind that it's not, it's better to resolve that dispute up front. This is true even if it might kill the deal now, rather than to have it surface a month or two later at the settlement table and kill the deal then. Make it non-assumable if you possibly can.

Some time ago, I heard figures stating that the average ownership of a house is approximately five years. When a home is sold, it will on the average be resold in five years. If your note is non-assumable then, the chances are very good that within five years, you will be paid the full amount regardless of the term of the note, because the present buyers will sell again at that time. Make the note non-assumable.

BUY AND SELL NOTES

Once you've taken back a note in lieu of cash for your equity in a house you've sold, what do you do then? Maybe your long term strategy is to hold several of these notes until the sum of the payments on those notes becomes an acceptable monthly income at which point, you can retire from your other job and live entirely on the income from rentals. That's a good plan, but, you are not limited to just that use of the notes you take back.

A note is an I.O.U. and I.O.U.'s are negotiable paper. In other words, you can buy and sell notes secured by real estate. Many investors do just that. Without the trouble of buying or selling real estate, without ever bothering with tenants, they simply buy someone else's paper and hold it until the balance comes due. You might want to sell some of your notes to one of these investors. You must remember, however, that in order to make that note attractive enough for an investor to buy, you must increase the yield of that note to the net effective interest rate that the purchaser of the note finds acceptable. This is done by discounting the face value of the note. This is an example of how it is done:

The person to whom you intend to sell the note requires a yield of 20% on his investment. If the interest rate on the face of the note is 15%, you will need to increase the net effective interest rate by 5% per year. If it is a one year note, then discounting the face value of the note 5% will arrive at the 20% figure that he has set for himself. Example:

Face Value	$10,000
Term	1 year
Interest Rate	15%
Desired Yield	20%
Discount	5%
Dollar Discount	$500
Sale Price	$9,500
Actual Yield	21.05%

If the note has a two year term, and the investor to whom you are selling the note needs 5% above the face of the note—that's 5% **per year** that you must discount it, for a total of 10%. The sale price of the note would be $9,000 in this example. The longer the term on the note, the more you'll need to discount it's face value in order to meet the net effective yield requirement of the potential purchaser.

Let's back up here for a second to the point where you are negotiating on the sale of your property in a case where you have an offer in hand requiring you to take back some paper. If you need to have the cash and have already gotten your ducks in a row by finding a purchaser for that note ahead of time, you can figure out very quickly how much you'll need to discount that note in order to sell it. If subtracting that discounted amount from the net proceeds of the sale of your house puts you below the amount you need to have, you might make one of the terms of your counter offer an increase in the sales price to reflect the amount you'll need to discount the note. If you are taking back a $10,000 note, for example, and you need to discount it $1,000 to sell it, add $1,000 to the sale price of the house. Also add $1,000 to the face of the note, and discount it $1,000 to your note buyer. Your net is the same, and since the additional $1,000 is paid in installments, you've only changed the buyer's offer by increasing his payment by $10 per month. He should be able to live with that.

WITHOUT RECOURSE

When you have the note in hand after the settlement of the sale of your house, and you go to convey it to the note buyer, you will need to endorse it just like you endorse a check. Remember these words: "Without recourse." Write them on the back of the note and sign your name immediately under those words. This language protects you against the buyer of the note who might seek to collect it from you, if the people who bought your house (the note makers) default on their payments. Since your name is still on the face of the note, the buyer of the note might otherwise feel justified in trying to force you to pay the payments in arrears, plus the full balloon immediately—all the full payment of

$30,000. Here's a suggestion: Make your change, take your notes back in two fives and two tens, but have them come due at different times. The parts of the "change" that you will want to spend should come due sooner. You might have one $10,000 note come due in five years, one $10,000 note come due in three years, but the $5,000 notes you can have come due in two years or less. You might reassure the maker of the note (if this idea fits into your long range plans— that you would be amenable to renewing the term of the note if you are still holding it and if he's in trouble when the note comes due. Don't write words to that effect on the face of the note, however, because if you do, you won't be able to sell it as readily.

WATCH TRUST POSITION

When you are negotiating to take back paper, you will be tempted to go for the highest interest allowable. In my state, deferred purchase money, taken back by the seller, is considered the same as a first trust for purposes of usury. Get a copy of that section of the state code, or ask an attorney by phone what usury laws apply to you. Don't get anywhere near usury.

The buyer will want the lowest payments he can get, and for purposes of a quick sale of your property, the lower the interest rate you offer, the better.

Never take less than a third position. In other words, never hold paper secured by a fourth or fifth trust. Also, only hold a third trust if you can be assured that there is sufficient value in the property to cover your interest if the property must be repossessed and sold quickly. The important word is "quickly." Without guarantees and insurance, banks seldom loan more than what the building could bring at auction—generally 80% of the market value. Neither should you loan your equity beyond some "quick sale" or auction value which is less than the market value of the property.

An investor friend of mine, in a rather speculative deal, sold a building and took a *seventh* trust position for part of his equity. Naturally, nothing is wrong with this sort of thing until something goes wrong with it. Something went wrong, and he had to foreclose and repossess his building. In his state, he was required to serve some notice to all trust holders senior to him in the land records. In four of the six trust positions senior to his, the notes had been sold, and in some cases sold twice. He was obligated to find all of the present note holders, scattered all over the state, before he could complete foreclosure and reclaim his building. You don't need that kind of trouble.

If the buyer of your property should default on a loan which is senior to yours, that note older will foreclose and you may need to pay off the balance of that senior trust in order to redeem your interest in the property. Otherwise, if the foreclosure sale does not bring enough money to pay back your interest, it is lost.

The more creditors in a senior trust position to you, the more likely you are to lose your money. If you won't be taking at least a third trust position, don't take paper back at all.

When you do hold paper that you do not intend to sell, don't be afraid to be creative. On a home that I sold, I accepted a third trust that paid zero interest for the first two years, interest accruing to the principal for the third year, and monthly payments of interest only for the fourth year. I tailored it to fit the buyer's needs, because that bird in the hand was worth several in the bush.

One other important thing that you can do with the paper that you hold is to borrow against it at the bank. Take your notes to the bank and allow them to hold the documents and collect the payments. Based on that collateral, many banks can give you a loan. Depending on the policy of the bank, they will loan up to a certain percentage of the face value of the note. The note is still in your name, because you've not sold the note to the bank, but you've recovered much of your cash. Remember that in order to have sold it, you may have had to discount it substantially to begin with, so this may be a very viable option.

Probably the most creative way to use the notes that you've taken back is to use them just like cash, at face value. Very often a seller will accept a note in lieu of a cash down payment. Once I bought a house with nothing more down than a note that someone had paid to me. I endorsed it over to the seller, and gave him the balance of the down payment in the form of an I.O.U. from me to him. I bought that house with no cash down, and, in effect, sold him the note that I had taken back at face value with **no discount**. The important thing to remember is that to be used this way a note should be drawn such that it is attractive to the seller to whom you intend to give it. It should pay a reasonable interest and be payable in a relatively short term.

There will be times when you will want to borrow against the equity that you have in a property, but won't be able to find a lender interested in lending to you against that property. That's all right, because you can lend the money to yourself. This is how it's done: Originate a note to "The Bearer." Secure it to the property with a deed of trust, and record the deed of trust. Take that bearer note to your investor, who buys notes, discount it and sell it. From that investor's point of view, this transaction is exactly the same as if you had sold the property taking back a note for your equity. You make payments to the note holder according to the face of the note.

A lot has been said and written, and will continue to be said and written about taking back paper. It facilitates, first of all, making a sale, where you otherwise might not be able to sell. It provides an income on an investment of cash that you never really had to begin with. Paper can be used to generate cash and also to leverage you into a transaction that you might not otherwise be able to get into.

My only caution is this: Don't take back paper unless it fits into your investment strategy. Then and only then, take it back on terms that fit **your needs** and **your purposes.**

Chapter 26

DON'T WHIP A DEAD HORSE

Recently, I toured an older home for sale that was in the process of being renovated by the owner. The owners, a young family, were doing most of the renovation themselves, despite the fact that most of the renovation was major. Walls were being taken out and moved around, plumbing was all being redone and wiring was being replaced. They had obviously put in an immense amount of work and money. The lady of the household was almost in tears as she showed us around the house, from one unfinished room to the next, from one bathroom that didn't work to another one with similar problems. We saw walls stripped down to the studs, a staircase with no banister rail and exposed wiring with no light fixtures.

It was apparent that they had lived in that construction site for some time because their furniture was still covered up with sheets. Construction material was leaning against the walls, and boxes of supplies were everywhere. There were ladders, paint buckets, drop cloths and plaster dust throughout the house. Under the prior owner, the building had been divided into four apartments. She told us that they had painfully and carefully taken out one wall after another to bring it to its present condition. It was obvious that they had gotten themselves into a project that was too large for their capacity. They were half way through the project, and didn't have the financial, technical, or emotional capacity to finish the job. Yet, here the house was on the market, priced well above what it should have been. Our agent told us that, although he had had several offers, the seller refused to take less than the listing price, because he didn't want to "lose money" on the deal. They were losing a great deal more than money already.

I thought to myself, "There is a man who doesn't know when to quit." There is such a thing as sending good money after bad. Remember the point of no return that I mentioned in another chapter. In any financial transaction, I believe there is also a point of no return; a point at which it makes no further sense to continue with the project. A loss is already assured and any further investment will only bring more loss. These people had found that point.

They hadn't realized it yet, but the time had come for them to stop trying to maximize profits and begin trying to minimize losses. A project of that sort can turn around very quickly from a money winner to a money loser. The longer you hold onto it, the more it will hurt you. Whipping a dead horse will not make it get up and run for you.

The family was working under a tremendous strain. Financially they could no longer afford to carry the property. They couldn't afford to finish the fix-up on it, and more importantly, they couldn't emotionally carry the property anymore. They were caught in a situation which I wish I had been able to counsel them against before it ever happened.

LIVING IN A CONSTRUCTION PROJECT

If at all possible, do not live in a construction project. I believe that people need order and structure in their lives, especially in their home lives. If the home life is unsettled or cluttered or confused, that same confusion and unsettled feeling permeates everything else that a person does. Although the immediate effect of that stressful situation may not be apparent from day to day, the long term effect is disastrous. Living around construction rubble and non-functioning facilities can't help but affect you adversely. In fact, the longer you are in that situation, the worse off you become.

If you buy a home to live in which is badly in need of repair, take the advice of one who has been there. Live somewhere else for a while until the house is in some degree of order; until you can unpack your bags, set up your furniture, and start living.

If you get into a project and discover that you don't have the money and can't get the money to finish it, don't put any more money or effort into it. Board it up and leave it if you must, but don't let it eat you up. **Don't whip a dead horse.**

We spoke in one of the last chapters about over-improving for the neighborhood, but there is such a thing as over-improving for the property, and also over-improving for your investment plans. Unless you want to go all the way in renovating a property and bring it, in a finished condition, up to the middle price range for the neighborhood, make as few improvements as possible. Sell it in a semi-improved condition. Sell its "potential" to someone who will pay to fill its potential. Make only those improvements which will indicate what can be done by the person who wants to spend the money to take it further. For instance, instead of carpeting the whole house, carpet a hallway. Rather than rewiring a house, replace a light fixture or two and instead of remodeling an entire kitchen, clean it and paint it. The goal for your purposes is to allow the prospective purchaser to see the potential. Let him make the investment. Take what profit you can without further investment. Don't throw good money after bad. Don't whip a dead horse.

Another reason for not going very far in terms of improvement, is that the cosmetic improvement you do make will probably be changed by the new owners anyway. They will be decorating and redecorating according to their own taste. I recall when we bought our last home, that what we saw of the sellers' taste in decorating did not appeal to us at all. The colors in the rooms were all wrong. They had put place-and-stick tile on top of hardwood floors and were busy wallpapering with paper that was not attractive to us at all. As a matter of fact, we told them to please not finish the wallpapering in the bathroom, because we would probably just take it down anyway.

They finished the papering in the bathroom, and we did take it down. We pulled the linoleum stick'em tile off the hardwood floors, and repainted all the rooms. In short, we undid at some expense to us, all of the decorating they had done at some expense to them. The actual value of that house to us was less in the redecorated condition in which we bought it, than it was before they did the decorating. We should have been justified in asking for a discount in the selling price for that reason.

When redecorating to show what can be done with a home, remember that you are appealing to the middle range of the bell curve of buyers for that neighborhood. Stay away from stylish, faddish, or theme decorating.

We all see homes that were built in a style that was stylish 20 years ago, or homes that are now decorated in a style that was stylish 20 years ago. Those same homes are very unattractive and unpopular now. Other homes that were built or decorated in a very conservative manner 20 years ago don't have any of the same disadvantages now of not fitting with our current styles and trends.

THEME ORIENTED DECORATING

When we were selling our own personal home, this point was well illustrated to us. I had taken great pains to decorate my son's room in an outdoor theme. I had built his bed up on a platform to look like a ranger station and had put up photographic mural wallpaper showing a beautiful panorama of forest. The ceiling we painted sky blue, and with wallboard joint compound, I made big swirls of clouds on the ceiling. During an open house, some lady went through and asked us if we had fixed the roof trouble. I explained that we had never had roof trouble and asked her what had given her the impression that we had. She said that in my son's room it looked like we had patched the ceiling. It was incredible to me that she hadn't seen the point of the whole room. I told her that those "ceiling repairs" were clouds. She didn't buy the house. I had to wonder how many others passed by our house because of the "roof trouble."

Stay away from any decorations or improvements which are theme oriented, stylish, or dramatic in any way. Those decorations and improvements will be distracting to as many people as they will be attractive to, taking the house out of the bell curve of buyers.

As a realtor, I was once working with a small builder, trying to sell his very expensive properties. He had lots of five acres each, on which he had built houses that should have been selling in the $300,000 range. They were in various stages of completion and this builder was in trouble. He needed to sell one or two of them under any terms just to get out from under the short term construction financing. This was during the period when the market had gotten so bad that there were few buyers, and fewer still in that upper price bracket. I asked him what he would do if he couldn't sell them, and he answered with something very interesting, "Then I'll bless the bank with them." That's an expression that has stuck with me since then.

There are conditions under which the prudent thing to do might be to "bless the bank" with the property. In other words, allow a bank to foreclose or grant the bank a deed of title in lieu of foreclosure. In commercial and large investment real estate, they call "blessing the bank with it" a "deed in lieu." This action gives the property to the bank, which would get it anyway after troublesome and expensive foreclosure.

DEED IN LIEU

There are several conditions which would indicate that a "deed in lieu" might be a reasonable alternative to taking a continuous or massive loss on a project. 1) The property may be overfinanced. In other words, the sum of all liens against the property is more than the market value of the property, or more than you can reasonably expect to receive from the sale of the property in the time frame in which you must sell it. 2) The property may become too run down, such that the renovations necessary would require borrowing so much money that the financing would be over what the property is worth. 3) When the owner cannot sell the property and his actual cash in the property has been very little, walking away from that cash investment is cheaper than continuing to carry the property. These would be situations which would indicate that "blessing the bank with it" may be reasonable.

There may be other reasons that a person would allow a bank to foreclose, but the basic reason behind it is that allowing foreclosure is less expensive on the bottom line than continuing to hold the property. It's purely a business decision.

Remember my reaction to my first threat of foreclosure "Hey, I'm not a bum or a drug addict or a crook. You can't foreclose on me." You may have the same emotional response if you are ever placed in that position. Foreclosure, although it is completely enshrouded with emotion, is not an emotional matter. It is purely a matter of dollars and cents. If the bank can get its money back or can minimize its losses sufficiently, it will foreclose. If you cannot meet your commitment to your lender, you will have no other choice but to face foreclosure. You may find it advantageous to offer the bank a "deed in lieu" or just let the bank take it over.

To guarantee that a buyer won't find it advantageous to walk away from a property, banks require a purchaser to bring some unborrowed cash into the purchase. If less than a 20% down payment is brought into the purchase in all cases except loans guaranteed by the government against loss upon foreclosure, the lender requires the borrower to pay for mortgage insurance to guarantee that the bank's exposure will be covered if he does walk away from it.

When banks or other lenders make loans for business purposes, they charge a higher rate of interest than they would to a non-business borrower. This is justified by the fact that there is additional risk. The business might fail and the debt might be uncollectible. That is a risk that the banks are willing to take under certain terms and with the increased return on their money. They are, in effect, sharing the profits of the venture, and also sharing in the risks of the venture. So, if a business project is terminated in disaster, the lenders will seek to regain their investment by seizing and selling what is left of the property of the business. Lenders protect themselves first, and foreclosure is the way they do it.

In the case that the auction price of a foreclosed house does not bring enough money to pay off the lender's outstanding balance, the lender can, in most states, seek from the court a "deficiency judgment" against other assets of the borrower. In a few states, the lender is not allowed to look beyond the foreclosed property to collect his money. In other states, the law limits how far the lender can go into the borrower's other assets to collect the balance of the funds owed after the foreclosure sale.

This fact is one good argument for keeping personal matters and business matters strictly separate. You might like to consider incorporating to spread the liability and keep your personal assets protected. Most professional people have incorporated themselves. Several attorneys I know are no longer Harvey Smutlap, attorney, but are Harvey Smutlap, Inc., or Harvey Smutlap , P.C. (private corporation), or are even Harvey Smutlap, Inc., Retirement Fund.

TAX INCENTIVES

There are certainly tax incentives for doing this, but Harvey Smutlap, attorney, is not the same person before the law as Harvey Smutlap, Inc. They both are capable of independent action and carry liabilities completely independently of each other. Doctors and dentists are also often incorporated, partly as a protection against malpractice suits and other liabilities.

Even without this protection, allowing foreclosure may be the answer to your financial troubles in your business dealings, and may be a reasonable alternative to facing continued loss.

FORECLOSURE & BANKRUPTCY

You may say, as I and others have, "But foreclosure will completely destroy me financially. It will ruin my credit for all time." That response is emotional, and I say that it "ain't necessarily so." Foreclosure, and for that matter, bankruptcy can be looked upon as remedies for an intolerable financial position. It may sound paradoxical that an action, which seems to destroy your financial standing, would actually be a remedy to help correct it, but I believe it is so.

Foreclosure and bankruptcy are not as disastrous as they may seem. I know people, who have gone through both and survived. They not only survived, but one comment that I frequently hear from them is that they wish they had done it much earlier, before their troubles had devastated them as much as they had. I was even told once, that it is easier to get credit after bankruptcy. The reason for this is that lenders know that for a period of several years (in my state, 7 years) you cannot declare bankruptcy again. They, therefore, will be able to collect their loans since bankruptcy cannot force them to take a loss.

I don't want to be accused of advising my readers to contract debts that they don't intend to pay. I do not believe that anyone should enter into a business obligation with the intention of defaulting. That is probably a good definition of fraud. I counsel strongly against anything that remotely resembles a fraudulent transaction. This entire chapter is motivated solely by the suffering I personally have gone through, and the suffering some of my friends have gone through over a long period of time, without realizing that a quicker and more merciful end is available.

Neither foreclosure nor bankruptcy is the end of the world, nor even the end of your investment career, but rather a detached, unemotional, dollars and cents, business decision.

The point of all of this discussion is: **Don't throw good money after bad. Don't whip a dead horse.** Minimize your losses and make your business decisions based on this bottom line: If it's less expensive to allow foreclosure, the best business decision may be to "bless the bank with it." Neither foreclosure nor bankruptcy is the end of the world. They may actually be the beginning of a better one.

Neither of those instances, foreclosure or bankruptcy, needs to interfere with your buying and selling real estate. One of the reasons, frankly, that many of the investors have gotten as far as they have is that in many transactions, their credit is never checked and their solvency is never questioned. As long as they continue to make their payments and meet their other contractual obligations, no one seems to care.